Basketball

Prentice-Hall International, Inc., *London*
Prentice-Hall of Australia, Pty. Ltd., *Sydney*
Prentice-Hall of Canada, Ltd., *Toronto*
Prentice-Hall of India Private Ltd., *New Delhi*
Prentice-Hall of Japan, Inc., *Tokyo*

DAVID H. STRACK
University of Michigan

BASKETBALL

PRENTICE-HALL, INC.
Englewood Cliffs, New Jersey

Photographs by Al Blixt, Jr.

Current printing (last digit):

10 9 8 7 6 5 4 3 2 1

Library of Congress
Catalog Card Number: 68-11345

Dedication

To my wife, Ruth Ann; and Sally, Julie, Lucy, Dave and Amy Strack.

To the players on the University of Michigan basketball teams of 1964, 1965, and 1966, whose inspiring play brought three Big Ten championships and national recognition in basketball to Michigan.

To assistant coaches Jim Skala and Tom Jorgensen and to trainer Jim Hunt, who played important roles in the development of these teams.

Preface

Basketball coaching is my profession, and I consider myself a fortunate individual to be coaching basketball at one of the nation's great universities—my alma mater, the University of Michigan.

From 1948 until 1959 I served as assistant basketball coach at Michigan under two very able mentors, Ernest B. McCoy and Bill Perigo. During the 1959-60 season I was fortunate enough to serve as basketball coach at another great state university, the University of Idaho. The greatest professional break I ever received was to be given the opportunity to become head coach at Idaho. The year I spent at Idaho was invaluable to me in terms of professional growth, and I will always have a warm spot in my heart for that great little school in the rolling hills of the Palouse. I will be forever grateful to Mr. Robert Gibb, former Athletic Director at Idaho, and Dr. Donald Theophilus, former president, who gave me this opportunity to become a head coach.

I also owe a debt of gratitude to Bill Orwig, athletic director at Indiana, who strongly recommended me to Idaho, and without whose recommendation I would never have gotten that assignment. I also owe a debt of gratitude to H. O. "Fritz" Crisler, athletic director at Michigan, who recommended to his athletic board that I be named head coach at the University of Michigan in the spring of 1960.

I only mention the above important events in my life to give some idea of the background and experience from which I derived the material for this book.

Frankly, I've never been besieged by requests from other coaches, high schools, junior high schools, and colleges to write a book on basketball. With the advent at Michigan of such great players as Bill Buntin, Cazzie Russell, Bob Cantrell, Larry Tregoning, Oliver Darden, George Pomey, and many others, and the subsequent success of our teams, I have found myself somewhat in demand as a clinic speaker. I must admit that after my first four years as a head coach, the only basketball clinic I conducted was at a girls' swimming camp. I am the first to admit that when the caliber of players I coached improved, my record in coaching took a decided turn upwards.

My reason for writing this book is that I just wanted to put down in writing my ideas on this great game. This book, in effect, explains how one basketball coach feels the game should be played. Admittedly, other teams have used some of our offensive and defensive maneuvers, our fundamental drills, and so on, but no one—to my knowledge—uses them exactly as we do.

During my first six years at the University of Michigan I had two very capable assistant coaches, Jim Skala and Tom Jorgenson. These two have contributed a great deal to my knowledge of basketball.

There are a great many intelligent, energetic, and competent basketball coaches in the United States and the world today. There are thousands of dedicated basketball players. Perhaps this book might be of some benefit to some of these people.

D. H. S.

Contents

ix

CHAPTER **1**

Philosophy

The dictionary defines *philosophy* as the beliefs, concepts, and attitudes of an individual or group. The beliefs, concepts, and attitudes of the basketball coach are of the utmost importance, and will be a determining factor in whether the coach is judged by his colleagues as being a success or failure.

As one matures in his chosen work, his philosophy also matures. At this particular phase of my own career there are certain definite beliefs and attitudes that I have concerning basketball. I have adopted these concepts through associations with many fine people, both in and out of the field of athletics—coaches, players, journalists, and successful people in all fields of life.

I am firmly convinced that words, thoughts, and hopes do not determine one's philosophy; but the way the basketball coach reacts to important human beings, players, associates, assistants, and the public provides an important insight into his philosophy.

The way in which the basketball coach reacts to various intangibles also provides information on his innermost thoughts. How does he honestly feel about the coaching profession, his attitude toward winning and/or losing, his concept of his part in the over-all picture of athletics? These impressions of the coach resolve important opinions in his thinking.

My own concepts, beliefs, thoughts, and reactions are as follows:

COACH AND PLAYER

The most important person connected with any basketball team is the player himself. It is the coach's duty to field the best team he possibly can, with the material he has at hand. He must be fair and objective in selection of this material. He must be a firm and honest administrator. Every coach starts with the respect of his personnel, but it is up to the individual, through his administration, to retain this respect. A basketball team, by its very nature (consisting of a coach and perhaps 12 to 15 players), is a close relationship—and the coach must realize this.

The head coach has to be the guiding authority. There can be no question of his judgment on anyone's part. *The coach's word is the absolute law.*

In my relationship with players at the University of Michigan, I have found the following practice very satisfactory. *I consider the first day of our practice to be the most important day of the entire year.* On this day I have a meeting with my entire squad, at which time we discuss the terms under which they, as players, will compete for the University of Michigan for the coming year. These are terms which I, as coach, set forth and which cover every facet of the game of basketball as I would like to see it played. We cover, in detail, our training rules and the way I expect our basketball team members to conduct themselves on the road. We go over the conduct of the players when we are appearing at home. We discuss, through these terms, their conduct in the academic classroom, and their general decorum on the campus. These terms, in my judgment, make it clear to the young men trying to compete on our basketball team that they have to make numerous sacrifices. However, these sacrifices are well worth the effort if they are to become members of our squad. At this meeting I give our team the chance to discuss these terms. Frankly, as coach and originator of these terms, I know they are fair and we rarely have any discussion of them. However, I do think it is wise that the players be given this chance to voice their opinion.

Once these terms are accepted they have no recourse but to follow them. This is the initial thrust of discipline—and no one can hope to achieve any semblance of success without a team disciplined both individually and collectively. I think it is extremely important for the coach to communicate with his players—to let them know that he is their friend, their consultant, their confidant. I, for example, want to know the problems which confront the players on my basketball team.

We do have one important rule, however; the player is not to bring any problem unrelated to basketball to me when our team is practicing. I firmly feel that, when we are practicing, the boy's concentration should be on that practice session 100 per cent. I do, however, want the boys on my basketball team to know that I have a sincere interest in their well-being. If the need arises, I want them to come to see me either at the office or at my home in order to bring to my attention any problem which they feel I might be able to assist them in solving.

Basketball is a game of such skill that if a boy is troubled mentally, as well as being troubled physically, it can have an adverse effect on his play. Consequently I think that the coach must be in a position to assist his young men in solving their problems, whether they relate to basketball or not. I feel very strongly that the crux of any basketball team is a strong coach-player relationship which is based on mutual respect.

The coach must respect each player on his team, and should never feel that his team would be better off without a particular player. Coaches are human and it is within the realm of possibility that some players are more appealing to him than others, but the coach must either respect each player on his team or be prepared to have serious morale problems.

COACH AND THE COACHING PROFESSION

The basketball coach must view his profession as noble and honorable. He must look upon the successful coaches as those men who have worked harder, organized more efficiently, planned better, and had the knack of developing winning talent. Never underestimate the value of excellent coaching. The word "luck" has no bearing on either the success or failure of any team or of any coach. I believe in two very old adages: (1) Luck is when preparation meets opportunity, and (2) The harder you work, the luckier you get.

I regard athletics as an extremely important extracurricular activity and an important part of our entire educational system. The basketball coach plays a major role in this vital work. The effective coach is one who realizes that he, in order to improve his own abilities, must continue to learn. Any coach who reaches the conclusion that he knows all there is to know about the game of basketball is going to be unsuccessful, and his team will become a very easy target for the opposition.

John Wooden, the very capable and successful basketball coach at U.C.L.A., stated at the conclusion of his 1964 season that he felt his team was a more effective team that season because he, himself, was a better coach in 1964 than he had been in previous years. This comes from a man who, in 29 years of coaching, had never experienced a losing season, and who, in 1964, won the national championship by compiling the amazing record of 30 victories and 0 defeats.

Coaching is a great profession, and the basketball coach should consider himself a privileged person and work to justify the faith that was put in him when he was appointed to his position.

COACH AND THE PUBLIC

The basketball coach must realize that athletics are an important part of the American way of life, and that the public (the fans) is not to be overlooked. A realistic approach must be taken by the basketball coach, and he must see that people's emotions are involved when his team (or any team) is playing. We, as coaches, are willing to accept the plaudits of the public when our team is victorious; conversely, we must be big enough to accept criticism when our team is on the wrong side of the ledger.

The coach has to view winning and losing realistically. Don't allow yourself to get an inflated or deflated idea of your own importance. The coach is important; however, the most important human beings connected with any team are the competitors.

COACH AND ASSOCIATES

The vital word in this relationship is *respect*. Many (if not most) of the techniques which I try to teach our basketball team at the University of Michigan have been adopted from other coaches. I have learned these techniques from fine basketball men at coaching clinics, from watching their teams play, or just listening to them talk basketball.

When our team at Michigan takes the floor against an opponent, I regard the opposing coach as a most worthy foe. I know that he is an intelligent, dedicated worker who will do everything within his power to defeat our team on this particular night. I think it is important for us to have a great deal of respect for our opponents, and yet not fear them.

COACH AND HIS ASSISTANTS

I served in the capacity of assistant basketball coach at the University of Michigan from 1948 until 1959; consequently I feel I can speak with some authority on the role of the assistant, and how I think the head coach should treat his assistants. I firmly believe it necessary that the head coach delegate certain definite responsibilities to his assistant coaches. This is not a difficult job, but it shows the assistant coach that he is an important part of the over-all basketball picture at your school.

Coaches are guilty of using the word *I* too much. In the vast majority of instances, it is the work of the head coach in communication with his assistant coaches which produces the winning combination. The relationship of the head coach and his assistants must be based on mutual respect and mutual loyalty. The head coach must listen to the advice and words of his assistants and weigh them carefully. Then, of course, it is up to him to either reject these ideas or incorporate them into the over-all scheme of things. If the head coach does incorporate the ideas of his assistant coaches, it is of the utmost necessity that these coaches be given credit for their contributions.

COACH AND OFFICIALS

Basketball, as played today, is a great game, a very fast game, a somewhat raucous game in which players, coaches, and fans spend themselves. And yet, very simply, it is a game in which two men (the officials) represent authority. The basketball coach must realize that the officials are an integral part of the game of basketball and deserve the coach's support.

I say, with complete sincerity, that basketball officials have never determined the outcome of a game in which my teams were competing. The coach must believe this, for it is true. Emotions do run rampant in this game of basketball, and the men "in the striped shirts" must be respected as what they actually represent—authority.

COACH'S REACTION TO WINNING AND LOSING

It is important that the coach take a realistic attitude toward winning and losing. We are a competitive nation. Competition has made the

United States the leading power in this world. It is important to win, and equally important for the coach to realize this and strive to accomplish this worthy goal.

The following quotation has been credited to a number of famous coaches in this country: "Winning is not the most important thing, it is the only thing." To me, this is a rather juvenile approach to this great question of winning and losing, and the coach's reaction to same. I would prefer to credit this quotation to some overzealous sportscaster or sportswriter.

If this quotation is taken at face value, it would imply that the coach would do anything to win—within either the legal or illegal realms—and that is not, in my opinion, an honest or realistic approach to the coaching profession. I would like to go on record as saying that winning is of the utmost importance, and that any coach worth his salt—or any coach worth that title—does everything within his power to see that his team comes out on the right side of the ledger. However, no coach wants to win at the expense of his players' health or his own dignity or honesty. These are things which I think the quotation indicates a coach might do.

I want each member of our basketball team, including players, coaches, and trainers, to be able to leave the floor at the conclusion of any game with no regrets, regardless of whether we have won or lost. If this is true, then each member knows that he has done his best. Collectively, as a *team*, we have done the best we can in playing, coaching, and planning for the game. There may well be a shared feeling of sadness if we have lost, but if each one has done his best there can be no regrets.

Our 1963-64 University of Michigan basketball team was captained by a young man named Bob Cantrell, and in that year Bob completed his third year of varsity play. Our 1963-64 team was successful in that it won 23 games and lost 5. However, Cantrell had played on two previous teams, the first of which, in the 1962-63 season, won 7 and lost 17. In all three years, win or lose, Bob Cantrell always came to me after the game and said, "Coach, I did my very best." That's the type of attitude I like in our players, and the type of attitude I think any coach should have.

One of the most important parts of my basic philosophy, relative to winning and losing, is that I never want any boy who plays for me to make an excuse when we lose. I am not looking for good losers on our basketball team; however, I want boys who take losses seriously. I think every coach should demand this of his team. It is easy in this day and age (and I fear it is done too much) to find a ready excuse why our basketball team, or our football team, or any of our teams, lost on a particular day. We can always blame the officials; we can blame the fact that our schedule has been too difficult and that we did not have enough time to prepare; or we can always go back and blame Old Lady Luck! Realistically, this is not the answer. The coach should never convey the idea to his players after a loss that they can reconcile that loss with an excuse. If the coach is prone to make excuses, then his players will make excuses. I have found from experience that the players can invent a few. Of course this is not an easy rule to follow, but I firmly believe that this rule has been as beneficial to me as any part of my coaching philosophy.

In reality, there is just one statistic which overpowers all of the rest— the final score. The coach, the team, the players who can take a loss in stride (as heartbreaking as the loss might be) are the type who will be successful.

The above words mirror my own reflections on this great game of basketball. I feel very strongly that any young man in the basketball coaching profession, at an amateur level, should have a definite philosophy and ideas on how he feels his team should operate. Don't be afraid to incorporate the great ideas you might pick up from other coaches into your own basic philosophy and approach to the game of basketball.

CHAPTER 2

Coaching Theory

GENERAL PRINCIPLES

It is important that the coach develop and believe in a particular style or system of play. This does not mean that he must be unique, or completely different from his colleagues, but that he, as a coach, thoroughly believes in and understands just what he is trying to do, both offensively and defensively. The thinking coach does not become stereotyped in his style of play; the personnel he has each year might dictate some changes. As he continues in his profession he must grow intellectually, continuing always to think and create and change if it is for the better.

I have never had the opportunity to coach in high school, a place—in my opinion—where some of the great basketball coaching is done in this country. I have, however, become acquainted with many successful high school coaches, gone into communities which have successful high school basketball programs, and observed the techniques of men who are at the helm of these successful programs. In these towns, big and small, where year after year the basketball program seems to be just a cut above the average, one can usually find the following situations.

The successful high school coach is dedicated to basketball. He thoroughly enjoys working with young boys, and does not worry or think about the number of hours he spends coaching basketball. He is one who believes that basketball is the greatest sport ever invented.

In this type of community the observer will find that the coach has made it possible for the boys of the town to play basketball—facilities are available, the parks have outdoor courts, and the gyms are open perhaps more than they are in neighboring towns or communities. The coach has seen to it that the boys are properly supervised. He has also made certain that the basketball program is started at the lower levels, so that the young boys in grade schools and junior high schools are interested in basketball and have an organized program at those levels. This requires work and great organization on the coach's part. Such a program might require great salesmanship to sell the school board and school administrators on the value of the basketball program in the junior high schools. However, it has proven to be a most worthwhile, satisfying, and beneficial experience both for the coach and for the young man participating in this program.

In the state of Michigan one of the most successful high school mentors is Lofton Green, of River Rouge, who has won more state championships than any other coach in our state. Lofton Green, in my judgment, meets all of the criteria which have been listed for successful coaching.

In the summer of 1964 I spoke at a number of clinics in Michigan. We held one in Ann Arbor when we played Duke University during the season, and Lofton Green was in attendance. There was a clinic at Windsor, Ontario, at which I spoke, and Lofton Green was in attendance. Late in the summer I spoke at Marquette, Michigan, in a clinic sponsored by the State High School Athletic Association, and Lofton Green was in attendance. I asked Lofton just why he attended all of these clinics when it was fairly obvious that I was giving approximately the same information at each one. His answer to me might be of interest to the reader. First, he enjoyed hearing anyone talk about basketball and enjoyed the association with the other coaches who were there. Second, he felt he might pick up some one thing which he could use the next season and which might get him a basket or two during the course of that year. Also, even if he did not pick up any new information, perhaps there were coaches in attendance whom he might be playing in the future and who might get some ideas from the speaker, so he wanted to be prepared for that eventuality. I use Coach Green as an illustration, for to me he epitomizes the successful basketball coach, and it has been my practice in my coaching career to study the teams and working habits of men for whom I have a great deal of respect and who have met with success in this interesting field of basketball coaching.

In my judgment, the successful basketball coach is one who is extremely well organized. No coach should attempt to lead his team in practice without definite organization plans. These plans would include a general one for the entire season. Much thought must be given by the coach to just what he hopes to accomplish in that season, and how he plans to go about accomplishing his objectives. At Michigan we first break our practice plans down into our pre-season work. At our level we have six weeks to prepare for our opening game, and try to get these weeks organized so that when the game competition begins we are prepared to do battle with the opposition. I realize that at the high school level there is not normally six weeks' time to prepare, which of course makes organization all the more important.

The real, and most important, organization plan is the daily one. It is imperative that the basketball coach organize each day's practice into minutes, and follow these plans to the minute. In this way, and this way only, will the coach be able to cover all of the practice area. I do not believe that there is any coach competent enough to practice just by ear. I have been told by some coaches that they feel it is impossible to organize and follow these plans to the minute, for things come up during practice which demand attention, and consequently the plans must be altered. I do not subscribe to this theory. We do follow our practice plans to the minute, and if something does come up that we feel needs more work we might change the next day's plan, which can, of course, be a flexible area. Organization is of the utmost importance. Everyone will agree that discipline of the basketball team is a key to success. Proper organization is an excellent way to begin discipline, both for the team and for the coach himself. The unorganized coach, the haphazard coach, is the one we would all like to play. Be organized!

OFFENSIVE THEORY

Without going into particulars of the various types of offense at this time, it appears that offensive style may be divided into three distinct categories:

1. The offense which puts the great and most important emphasis on the fast

break, with the fast break being the most important offensive weapon of the team.

2. The offense in which the team controls the ball and manipulates players so as to always get the high percentage shot. In other words, a controlled ball offense.

3. A third offensive plan could be called a combination of both; that is, one which utilizes the fast break when it presents itself, and also uses the controlled ball of the disciplined type of offense when it is necessary.

Fast Break

A coach who believes in the fast break type of offense as his basic plan of attack feels that his ball club will get more shots and better shots by attacking quickly, before the defense is set. The nature of this offense is to overpower the opposition offensively with speed and shooting. This offense has been used very successfully by many great basketball coaches. The idea is just to outscore the opponent—and who can say that's a bad idea!

Advantages

1. The team can score quickly.
2. Demands great conditioning on the part of the boys playing it, and if run well demands great ball handling.
3. The nature of this game is that the young men like to play it.
4. This type of game is pleasing to the spectator.
5. The fast break demands action, and action is what has made basketball the great spectator sport that it is today.

Disadvantages

1. Although the fast break is based on sound fundamentals, by nature it can lead to more errors; that is, giving up the ball without a shot—and a team which runs wild and shoots wild can become disorganized.
2. A strong defensive basketball team, and a basketball team which has great strength in its rebounding, can throttle this offense before it gets a chance to start.
3. If the opposition succeeds in stopping the break, chaos can become the order of the day, as patterned basketball, or controlled basketball, is something not understood or liked by players who have been coached just to run and shoot.
4. The basketball is often shot without any offensive board coverage.
5. This type of basketball demands the big, strong, better brand of basketball players, and the coach who uses it as his basic offensive weapon must have these players.

Control Ball

This is a very disciplined type of game, and one that the players must be sold on. The basic idea is to always get a high percentage shot, always have board covered, always have floor balanced. The purpose is not to try for a great many shots, but to take only the high percentage shot. This would be a percentage game, and the fast break is used rarely, if at all.

Advantages

1. This type of game can diminish errors.
2. Patience is taught by playing in this manner.
3. The team can get (if properly trained and patient) a good percentage shot.
4. It can lead to a team disciplined in action and thinking.
5. Games can be won with perhaps a shade less in the way of natural talent.
6. This kind of play is usually coupled with great defense.

Disadvantages

1. Players, generally, would rather play a faster game.
2. Patience is really needed.
3. It is difficult to score many points quickly if needed.
4. An intelligent crowd is needed to appreciate this kind of play.
5. Offense of this type needs a strong-minded coach, which could be an advantage.

I respect the right of any coach to manipulate his men offensively and defensively in any manner which the rules permit. I do not, however, believe that this slow-down type of basketball contributes to the overall betterment of the game. Our game is great because of its action, maneuverability, shooting, and running. I honestly feel that the coach who teaches a true, never run, control type of game takes advantage of the game of basketball and the fact that the very high percentage of coaches prefer action. I want to re-emphasize that, although I don't agree with this style of play, I respect the coach who uses it.

**Controlled Fast Break
and Controlled Set Offense**

This offense is a cross between the two mentioned previously. The basketball team which is coached to run when the opportunity presents itself and is smart enough to control the ball when necessary will obtain maximum efficiency from its players. This brand of action basketball eliminates the prime disadvantages of both previously described systems and combines the advantages of both.

1. This system does not mean that you "put all your eggs in one basket," but rather that you hedge somewhat to utilize the best combination available.
2. This system does demand great discipline and still utilizes natural talents of the players. It also allows a team to take advantage of the opposition's weaknesses.

Again, emphasis must be on the coach's being absolutely sure in his own mind that what he is doing is correct—100 per cent correct! This confidence will rub off on his team, as they must be equally sure of what they are doing. Know what you (as coach) want to do, and then work hard enough and be patient enough to do it.

I would like to emphasize something in which I strongly believe: it is not any particular system or style of play which will guarantee success, nor is it X's and O's and diagrams of maneuvers. Assuming that every coach has equal material, equal facilities, equal practice time, equal luck or lack of bad luck, the coach who is successful is the one who best *prepares* his team *to do battle with the opposition*. If there is any secret to successful basketball coaching it is in the preparation of the team to play its schedule.

Coaching is a most important factor in winning. I do not believe that any coach on any level can win with inferior players, but to me, the successful coach, when blessed with fine players that he has developed or recruited, motivates these players to operate at maximum efficiency, individually and collectively. At the University of Michigan we strive to have a team which is both happy and efficient. When these two elements combine with talent, it makes for a pleasant season.

CHAPTER **3**

Fundamentals

Fielding H. Yost once made the statement that the two most important items in victory were fundamentals and morale. The team which is fundamentally sound and has high morale is a difficult team to defeat.

No athlete in any sport completely masters all fundamentals, but the great athlete continually strives for mastery. There is no easy way for a basketball player to become fundamentally sound, nor is there any short cut for the coach in teaching fundamentals. Both player and coach must work diligently, pay attention to each detail, have patience, and strive to improve.

At Michigan, we do feel there are certain important aspects in the teaching of fundamentals, and our coaches follow these rules:

1. *Blow a sharp whistle.* This means that when we blow the whistle to get the attention of our club at practice, we want that attention immediately—if not sooner! The players must respond at once and give the coach their immediate and undivided alert attention.

2. *Explain.* The coach must realize that he is dealing with alert and intelligent young men, and consequently must be practical and realistic in his teaching. Each fundamental, pass, shot, or movement must be explained simply and concisely to the players, and they must be told how this particular maneuver will fit into your over-all plan.

3. *Be simple.* Basketball is not a complicated game. In effect, the coach tries to teach his players to do two things very well—score and prevent the opposition from scoring.

4. *Demonstration and teaching.* You must know exactly what you wish to accomplish. Correct teaching equals correct habits, and winning basketball is a game of correct habits.

5. *Demand speed.* From the very first drill we demand that our fundamentals be run at top speed. We will sacrifice precision for speed, because half-speed precision is worthless. Basketball demands speed in all fundamentals, and there is no place for half-speed in successful basketball.

6. *Generate enthusiasm.* The learning process involved in fundamentals is a difficult one, and the coach must provide genuine enthusiasm. In my judgment, genuine enthusiasm is the greatest intangible asset a player can have. Enthusiasm supplies the force which generates the momentum in the drive for victory. Without enthusiastic teaching and response the cause is pretty well lost. I don't mean to imply that everyone has to enjoy every minute of every practice, but if anything is to be accomplished, coach and players must respond positively.

7. *Be disciplined.* The coach *must* be an honest disciplinarian. Demand perfection and 100 per cent performance in practice, and you are assured of this type of effort in the game. Get rid of the laggards who will not pay the price for victory.

8. *Be organized.* Know to the minute how you plan to conduct each practice. This is the only way you can accomplish all you must in covering each and every fundamental and each and every detail needed to prepare your team.

Remember, the fundamentally sound team has a tremendous advantage over all others. Fundamentals are the coaches' responsibility, and the value of the coach who can school his team skillfully in all of the fundamentals is inestimable.

We group our fundamentals into five categories, and strive to have our players master the drills involved in the teaching of each one. We want our drills to be simple, functional, beneficial, and effective.

GROUP I: BODY CONTROL

As stated, we run all of our drills at top speed, and these drills are used primarily to teach a boy to move efficiently in all directions (right, left, forward, back), correctly and without the ball. It is important to note that if one player has the ball his fair share of the time, he'll possess it 10 per cent of the time of a game. This means that 90 per cent of the time he will not have the ball, so he'd better learn to play and move without it.

What we try to accomplish is speed movement in all directions. We continually work to increase speed and quickness. We want quick starts, stops, change of direction, and great body balance at all times. Basketball is a game of quickness, and this can be coached and a player's maneuverability efficiency increased through various body control drills.

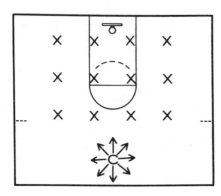

Hands Up Drill.

1. Place players approximately five feet apart across the floor and have them take a defensive stance position with one foot leading and the same hand up in the air. The other hand and forearm are parallel to floor.
2. Knees must be flexed, back straight, head and eyes up, and the weight evenly balanced on both feet.
3. The coach starts and gives verbal and hand commands, left, right, forward, or backward.
4. The players change hands only on coach's order. We also have players lead this drill on occasion.
5. During the first month of practice we use this drill daily. We start at two minutes per hand, or four total minutes, the first day of practice, and conclude one month later at seven minutes per hand, or fourteen total minutes.
6. As a coach, I feel that this drill, if run properly, can accomplish many things, such as:
    (a) Great conditioner for team.
    (b) Teaches correct position. Coach must demand correct position even when fatigue sets in.
    (c) Teaches correct defensive moves, vertical and lateral moves.
    (d) Strengthens shoulders and arms.
    (e) Lets players know immediately that basketball is a difficult game to play physically and those who don't want to work should get out.

Jim's Drill

This drill was invented by Jim Skala, assistant basketball coach at the University of Michigan.

1. We line our players up on the base line. At the whistle they will do the following:
   (a) Run to mid-court line.
   (b) Double back to foul line.
   (c) Reverse to base line at opposite end of court.
   (d) Reverse to mid-court.
   (e) Reverse to foul. line.
   (f) Run for original base line.
2. Options on this drill are to give them a ball and have them dribble, changing hands with each change of direction.
3. Keep players facing in one direction so that they may practice quick changes of direction and running backwards.
4. We end many of our practices with this drill. The number of times we run it is up to our (coaches') discretion, and is determined by hard work, or lack of it, by the team.

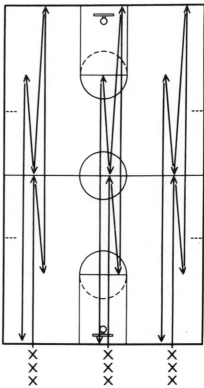

Jim's Drill. This diagram shows direction and distances run by each player.

Moby's Drill

This drill was picked up from our baseball coach, Moby Benedict.

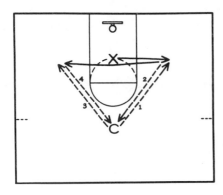

Moby's Drill.

1. This drill is designed for just one player. The player lines up directly in front of the coach (15 feet) or person the coach designates.
2. The coach rolls ball at a 45° angle and player slides to get it, passes ball back, and returns to center.
3. Coach then rolls ball to other side.
4. Coach keeps this up as long as he wishes, but again must demand correct stance defense from player. Do not allow fatigue to change this position. This is physically a tough drill and that's why we like it.

Slides and Sprints

We start our practice by having our players run slides and sprints in order to get ready to play, and also to introduce an element of fatigue. The drills we use in this part of our practice are as follows, with the time varying, depending upon the situation, from three to ten minutes. As the season progresses, we reduce the time spent on these drills, but we do start our practice, except the day before and after we play a game, with them.

1. We start by jogging from base line to base line and returning, then we sprint two laps.
2. We then slide laterally down and back while facing in one direction, which of course makes the player move in two directions. In this, we stress correct position, knees flexed, head and eyes up, back straight, forearms parallel to floor, and back straight.

3. We stress a great deal of backward running. The good basketball player is one who can motor backwards under control.
4. We pair off our team, having two boys face each other on the base line. They move in twosomes down the court, base line to base line. One player keys on the other. Both slide laterally down the court with the primary player changing directions periodically, which makes the one keying on him change also.
5. Also using two men, we have one just run at the other boy, who must stay in front running backwards. As the runner changes direction and speed the defender changes direction and speed, staying in front and running backwards. One player defends for 94 feet, then they turn around and switch positions.
6. We then give one player a ball and run the same drill as in 5, only the runner dribbles. We first make the defender stay in front with his hands behind his back. We stress keeping head and shoulders in front of the dribbler. We do not go to score on this drill.
7. We also put the player without the ball on the side of the dribbler. We have the dribbler dribble base line to base line and the other player keep up by sliding laterally. The dribbler changes speed and direction, but only in a straight line. When dribbler accelerates, the slider *runs* and catches him, and then resumes slides.

In summarizing our body control drills, I would say they are not our players' favorites. In other words, they dislike the slides, backward running, and so on. I've found that the drills our players dislike most are the most productive conditioners, and so we use them a great deal.

Everyone agrees that it takes a player in superb physical condition to play 30 or 40 minutes of tough basketball. It's my firm conviction that the well conditioned player can go a complete game. I am also convinced that great condition and endurance are not only physical but mental. We strive to teach our players *not* to give in to themselves when they become fatigued.

The basketball coach who can get his players into the right physical condition and frame of mind to sell themselves for as long as they are called on to do so has a tremendous jump on his opponents.

GROUP II: DRIBBLING

The second fundamental we are going to discuss is dribbling. The dribble is an important phase of basketball, and we want our players to understand the dribble and to use the correct techniques while dribbling, to know when to dribble and when not to dribble, and the advantages and the disadvantages of dribbling. Our drills are simple, emphasizing both speed and control.

There are four game or scrimmage situations in which it is feasible to use a dribble:

1. Advance the ball when you cannot pass.
2. Clear ball from defensive backboard.
3. The offensive player beats his man and dribbles hard for goal and a layup.
4. Dribble in order to clear the ball from a congested area.

The disadvantages of the dribble are as follows:

1. Allows one player to dominate the ball too much. When this happens, the other four players begin to stand around.
2. The dribble has very little utility in the normal offensive plan, and practically none in ours. Actually, a dribbler ruins many team offenses.
3. The dribble is the slowest method of advancing the ball and breaking and scoring opportunities are sometimes ruined because of a dribble.

Our dribble drills are conducted with the idea of teaching both the speed dribble and the low protective dribble. With the low dribble, we emphasize the outside hand dribble in order to keep the body between the ball and the defensive man. We want the knees flexed, body relaxed and in a protective crouch, head and eyes up, and peripheral vision used. We do not want the ball slapped into the floor, but the fingers on the hand should be spread and should control the ball and the dribble with a slight wrist action.

We do not emphasize the dribble, and therefore we do not have many drills. We do not feel that the dribble is an effective way to delay or stall. Naturally, many of our drills utilize the dribble, but there are only two drills we actually call dribble drills.

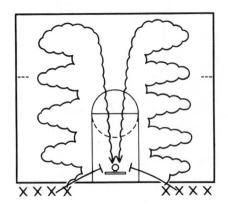

Low Dribble—High Dribble. 1. Two lines of players are on the base line. The leader of each line dribbles low and controlled to mid-court, changing speeds, direction, and dribbling hands. This is our protective low dribble.

2. When the dribbler reaches mid-court, he turns and comes dribbling high and as hard and as fast as he can for the basket to score a layup.

3. A coach stands under the basket and tries to harass this shooter by shouting, faking at him, or even fouling him. We want the shooter to learn to ignore the opposition and score, and, if fouled, convert the three-point play.

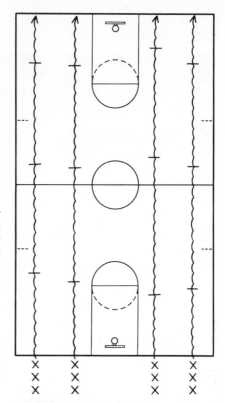

Dribble Reaction Drill. 1. We divide our team into four groups. Front man in each group has a ball and dribbles hard for opposite end on a whistle command. The coach will blow his whistle and the dribblers must stop at once and pivot away from an imaginary pursuer. The player starts on succeeding whistle and reacts to each whistle in same manner.

2. We hope to sharpen our players' reflexes and improve their reactions. We hope, by this drill, to eliminate the play in which our player dribbles ball, stops quickly, and fumbles ball to opposition.

Cazzie Russell, Michigan. High-speed dribble and drive for goal, using outside left hand.

Rich Falk, Northwestern. Protective dribble. Note defensive position of Cantrell of Michigan.

Oliver Darden, Michigan. Low protective dribble using outside hand.

GROUP III: BALL HANDLING—PASSING AND RECEIVING

It's difficut to make the statement that any one fundamental is of greater importance than any other. However, the truly great players like Cousy, Robertson, Bradley, and Russell have all been exceptionally fine ball handlers. We've isolated our ball handling drills just to include those which train our players to pass and receive the ball correctly. Again, simplicity is stressed, and we do feel that our drills increase the ball handling efficiency of our team.

We want our players to understand various rules we have in passing the basketball, which are:

1. The closer the defensive man is to you the easier it is to get the ball by him. Do not try to pass the ball by your defensive man if he's dropped off you. Move up to him.
2. Pass the ball so it hits your receiver in the area between his shoulder and waistline.
3. Study your defensive man. You should be able to *read* him after a few minutes and play your passes and other offensive moves according to his strengths and weaknesses.
4. Throw crisp passes, keep eye on target, and follow through.
5. Do not try to execute fancy or hope passes. These only give aid and comfort to the enemy.
6. Understand various passes and when to use the different types which are practiced. These types are two handed chest, two handed overhead, one handed flip, bounce, baseball, and shovel. The coach does his job if he can make a player understand why one pass is better than another in certain situations.
7. The passer must know and believe in one fundamental idea: If a pass is thrown and not completed, it is the receiver's fault. *Pass accurately.*

Our basic rules in receiving the basketball are as follows:

1. Be sure to look the ball into your hands.
2. Receive the ball with fingers spread and the hands relaxed.
3. Believe in and abide by the following fundamental rule: If you receive an errant pass, regain complete control of yourself and the ball before you attempt to throw another pass. Do this and *one bad pass will not beget another.*

The basic passing and receiving drills we use follow.

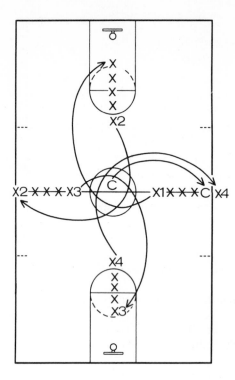

Manipulation Drill (Four Corner Drill). Coach (C) starts in middle and moves left, with good defensive shuffle. He hits X1, X1 hits C back, and C hits X1 right back as he makes semicircle to back of X1's line. This is repeated until all X1's are X2's, X2's are X3's, and X3's are X4's, and X4's are X1's. It teaches the boy ability to handle feet, eyes, arms, hands, and wrists, and to pass and receive ball correctly. It is a fine drill for fast break precision passing. The moves of each player are shown. Passes are not shown for the sake of clarity, but we use a two handed chest pass exclusively in this drill.

In File Drill. Players remain in file—they pass to front man in opposite lane while travelling at a fast rate of speed. The receiver must pass the ball immediately to a man running at him. The passer steps toward goal and runs hard around coach, who stations himself at base line. He passes and then runs for back spot in the line opposite the one from which he started. It becomes a type of figure eight drill.

We also have the coach pass the ball to the player breaking by him, and the player returns the ball to the coach. This means the player passes and receives ball three times each during one full circuit. We feel this drill teaches players to pass and receive ball on the move. It is also a conditioner when half the court is involved. The coach must emphasize speed in running. The pass must be a soft one.

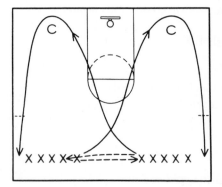

Pepper Drill. Place one player 10 to 12 feet from four or five others. Keep two balls moving back and forth. Speed in passing is emphasized. This builds wrists and fingers of the man in front. It is also a good peripheral vision drill.

Ball Hounding Drill. Team lines up at center court. Coach has the ball one side, and as players break for goal the coach makes a bad pass, rolls the ball, and so on, to driving player, who has to receive ball, regain balance and control, and go to score. We feel this drill teaches the player to handle a bad pass and regain control of himself and the ball. Every time a pass is thrown and received, it is necessary for the player to do these two things correctly, so we are constantly striving to reach an optimum degree of perfection in these categories.

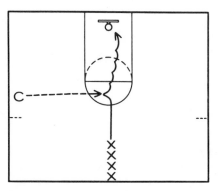

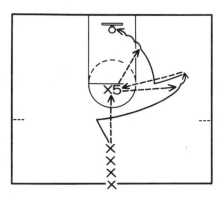

High Post (Change of Direction Drill). Team lines up behind X1 and post man X5 is at high post. X1 hits X5, heads in one direction, changes and goes to side of court at foul line extended. X5 returns ball to X1. X1 hits X5 and follows, but changes direction abruptly, drives for goal, receives pass from X5, and continues in and scores.

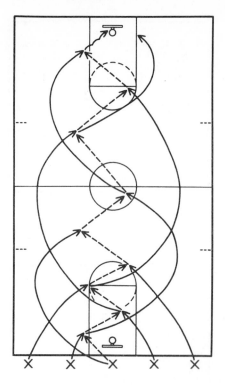

Five Man Running and Passing Drill.
Five men are on the base line. The ball is
in the middle and we pass and go behind·
two men weaving down the court. We run
this until all five men score.

Three Line Out (High Post). Divide
team into three lines out. X2 has ball, hits
X3 and heads for high post position (two
handed chest pass). X3 passes two handed
overhead cross court pass to X1. X1 hits X2
at high post and cuts (flip pass). X2 returns
ball to X1, cutting, and X1 passes back to
X2 immediately. X3 double cuts off X1's
tail and receives pass from X2. X3 continues to cut with ball, stops, pivots, passes
to X1 on opposite side of basket (shovel
pass). X1 hits X2, who cuts hard from high
post, and X2 scores. There are eight passes
in this drill and all must be executed correctly or the maneuver fails. X2 may start
pass to either side.

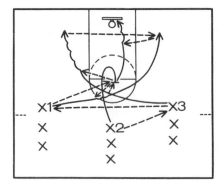

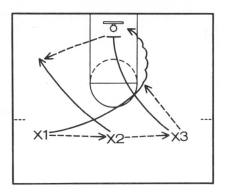

Three Line Out (Continuity Drill). Divide team into three lines out. X1 passes to X2 and cuts for goal. X2 passes to X3 and goes to corner on X1's side. X3 passes to X1 cutting for goal, and X1 shoots. X3, after passing to X1, goes for basket, rebounds shot, passes to X2 in corner. X2 snaps ball back to next man in X1's line and movement is started again. X2 goes to rear of X1's line, X3 to rear of X2, and X1 to rear of X3.

This drill enables us to work on hitting a man moving for the basket, rebounding and clearing to the corner, and snapping the ball from the corner to a man up the floor.

Sometimes we incorporate this drill in our break drills by starting the three men under the basket, weaving them to mid-court, reversing, and driving to score with this drill. Then we rebound and run full court to opposite basket, utilizing one of our break drills.

GROUP IV: REBOUNDING

For two seasons, 1963-64 and 1964-65, our University of Michigan team led the Big Ten Conference in rebounding. This was due to a great extent to our personnel, who were big, strong, aggressive, and fearless. These two teams were led by Bill Buntin, 6' 7", 235 pound center, Oliver Darden, 6' 7", 220 pound corner man, and Cazzie Russell, 6' 5", 215 pound guard. This triumvirate constituted an awesome sight to our opponents, but a most pleasant sight to our coaching staff.

Our teams at Michigan have been strong rebounding clubs because we stress rebounding and encourage an aggressive, clean type of ruthlessness on the boards. We praise strong boardwork, and find little use for the player who does not like to rebound and play the game with pride and a sort of controlled abandon.

Unfortunately, there is no simple, easy, surefire way to teach rebounding to young players. We have a few simple drills which we think accomplish what we wish with rebounding. As coaches, we try to sell our team, our rebounders, on one idea: when anyone on our club shoots, the rebounders must *go to the board*. We continually stress this by shouting, instructing, encouraging, demanding that our team go to the board, go to the board.

I feel that our offense releases players at the right spots to rebound, and all they must do is *go to the board* and get the ball if it misses. On the offensive board we like to keep the ball up close to the ring by tapping it back up when it misses. On the defensive boards we want to grasp the ball firmly and take it away from that board.

We emphasize and demand from our team that everyone be able to assume the responsibilities of rebounding. We stress the following ideas relative to rebounding:

1. Correct positioning means that the player must have his knees flexed and be ready to leap for the ball. In close to our basket we block the offensive man off the boards.
2. The first responsibility of our players is for each one to *keep his man off the backboard.*
3. We stress leaping for the ball from the knees' flexed position. The player's arms should be outstretched and the ball *snapped* from the board. Our rebounder's wrists should roll away from his body, which automatically keeps the ball away from his chest. We want our players to try and scrape the board with the ball—this insures proper hand and wrist action.
4. When the player lands on the floor his feet should be apart, knees flexed, elbows bent, and hands squeezing the ball.
5. An immediate pass to an outlet man is desirable. If this is not possible, we want our player to clear the board by dribbling away from it.
6. We stress that when our player goes after the ball on either board, he goes after the ball as if his life depended on getting it. We want our boys to go for the ball and get it regardless of whom they encounter on the way— friend, foe, or referee!
7. Second effort is imperative in rebounding. On the offensive board a good second effort keeps the ball in play and results in many a two points. On the defensive board, great effort limits the opposition to one shot. Our maximum of one shot per possession for the opponents, and a minimum of one shot for us, is our rebounding goal.

Rebounding Drills—Defensive

We also run a five man defense and break maneuver designed to clear the defensive board quickly and fast break. In my early years of coaching I thought you could run five man realistic patterns for a five man break, but I do not now believe this is possible.

We stress getting the ball out quickly and filling up the three lanes. We want all five of our men to break; the first three attack the whole way, the fourth looks to see if he can be a trailer, and the fifth remains a safety man.

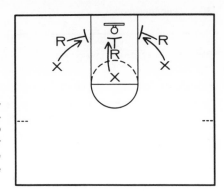

The coach stands under the basket and, on the whistle, R, who has been facing X, turns, plants himself, and blocks out X, who is charging straight to the board. We want contact here and teach our rebounders the correct position for keeping the offensive men out.

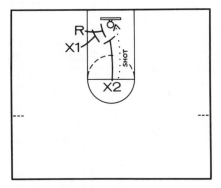

Coach passes ball to X1, and he and X2 and X3 rotate until one shoots, then all six pound for the ball.

X2 shoots and R rebounds. X1 and X2 then clamp R and try to prohibit his pass out. This is an effective drill as many teams try to stop their opponent's fast break at their own backboard.

Rebounding Drills—Offensive

Remember—games are won and lost on the backboards (an old but true axiom). Basketball players are becoming quicker, stronger, better leapers, and more courageous. We try and insure ourselves that our rebounders measure up in each category.

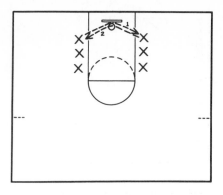

We have our front line man tap the ball back and forth over the hoop. Each man handles or taps the ball ten times.

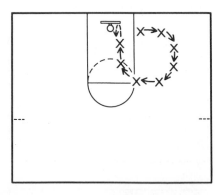

We circle our team first on our side and then on the other, and the players are instructed to keep the ball on the board and never let it hit the ground.

#22, Bill Buntin, Michigan. Strong rebound vs. Minnesota. Note full arm extension.

#22, Bill Buntin, Michigan. Rebounding and blocking opponent from ball. Note hard position ball from body.

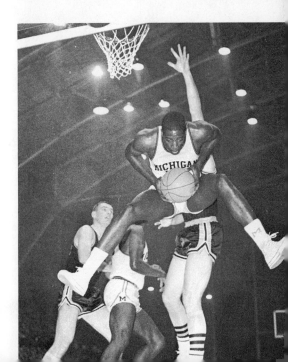

Oliver Darden, Michigan. Defensive rebound vs. Minnesota.

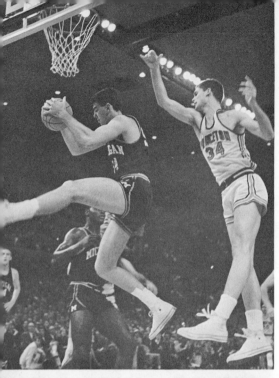

Jim Myers, Michigan. Defensive rebound vs. Princeton.

Oliver Darden, Michigan. Defensive rebound vs. Michigan State.

32

Bill Buntin, Michigan. Defensive rebound vs. Ohio State. Rebound with abandon.

Bill Buntin, Michigan. Offensive left-hand tap vs. Northwestern.

GROUP V: SHOOTING

Basketball is actually a very simple game. The primary object is to put a ball, which is approximately 10 inches in diameter, through a hoop which is 18 inches in diameter, and is suspended 10 feet from the ground. All of the fundamentals we teach are geared to help accomplish this goal. All of our team offensive maneuvers are designed to make this job easy. Scoring is the name of the game; consequently, shooting techniques and shooting fundamentals have to be catalogued as the most important of all of the fundamentals.

At the University of Michigan we have certain basic ideas on shooting the basketball which I would like to share with you. As in our other four fundamentals we do stress, or attempt to stress, simplicity. We strive to improve our players' shooting accuracy by instilling correct habits through constant practice. There is no easy way to improve a player's accuracy, nor are there any easy ways to teach anyone to shoot a basketball with a reasonable degree of accuracy. Correct fundamentals and constant practice are the only ways the young player—or any player— can become a proficient basketball scorer.

Robin Freeman, who was at Ohio State in the middle 1950's, led the nation in scoring and was one of the most accurate shooters that basketball has known. By his own admission, he shot a basketball during his formative years in high school and in college a minimum of 500 times per day, 365 days a year.

Bill Bradley, the great Princeton All-American of 1963-64-65, stated that anyone could become very proficient in basketball shooting if he is willing to spend a minimum of two to three hours per day, every day of the year. Bradley did this in his home town, summer and winter, and would shovel the snow out of his driveway in order to make room to continually toss the basketball at the hoop.

Cazzie Russell, Michigan's great All-American, did not just suddenly become a very accurate shooter. Once he started playing basketball (and actually he did not start until his freshman year in high school), he spent a great deal of time each day with the ball.

The great shooters of the game have not just confined their shooting to the months of October through March, but have spent time shooting the basketball practically every month of the year and practically every day in each month.

We try to break our shooting down into two distinct characteristics. One is the physical characteristic which we wish our players to have, and the other is the mental characteristics so important to the good shooter. On the physical side we think the position of the hands on the ball is of the utmost importance. The ball should rest on the outstretched fingers of the hands and must also rest on the butt of the hand. We do not believe in shooting exclusively from the fingertips, as I do not think that the average young player can control the ball from just his fingertips. I do feel that the ball, as it leaves the hand, must be propelled finally by the fingertips; hence, fingertip control is stressed as being of vital importance. The initial contact of the ball in the right hand, for a right handed shooter, should be on the fingertips and on the butt of the hand, but the palm of the hand should not touch the ball.

For the right handed shot, we feel that the right hand should be behind the ball and the left hand the steadying influence on the basketball. Whether the player is shooting a set shot, a foul shot, or a jump shot, the initial hand position should be the same.

The position of the arms and elbows is also of the utmost importance. The elbows should be in, and almost at a 90° angle with the floor. We do not like to have the elbows cocked out at an odd angle, as we feel this makes the hand position incorrect.

The follow through on any shot in basketball is also of basic interest. We stress, very strongly, hand, arm, and eye coordination. We want our players to view the front edge of the basket (if they are shooting directly at the hoop, as against shooting a bank shot, so to speak). Their eyes are to remain on their target either until the ball has passed through the net or they are certain that the shot has been missed. This is necessary in order to insure the correct follow through.

We stress that the arm be fully extended when the shot is released. Once the ball has left the fingertips of the hand we would like to have our players follow through and, from a full arm extension, make sure that the wrist is broken down and to the outside, with the fingers stretched out and pointing down. We feel that this guarantees the follow through. We do not want the boy to shoot the shot and jerk his hand back toward his head the minute the ball leaves his hand, nor do we want him to follow the ball in flight. Players have asked what difference it makes if, once the ball has left the hand, the eyes follow the ball in flight. It's been my experience, however, to note that the eye on the ring insures the follow through and the correct shot; therefore, the eye on the ring is of great importance.

In discussing the jump shot, which has revolutionized shooting, we stress the following fundamentals in addition to the previously discussed hand, arm, and eye coordination. We do not demand that our players jump as high as they possibly can before releasing the shot. The jump shot is a great weapon, not because of how high the player jumps, but just because he does jump and the defensive man does not know when he is going to jump. We do want the shot released at the top of his jump, with the correct hand, arm, and eye coordination.

Since there are so many variations in jump shooters' styles, we do not demand any particular style from a player using this shot, although we do stress the standard shooting fundamentals. Some of our players shoot jump shots from the forehead, some shoot from above the head, and if a player shows a good degree of accuracy in this shot we do not change it. Of course, if a player is unusually accurate in shooting any kind of a shot we will not change his method.

We stress quickness in shooting the basketball, and all of our shooting drills stress quickness. The only time in the game of basketball that the ball may be shot at the player's leisure, so to speak, is during the foul attempt. Any other time the ball must be shot quickly and accurately and, usually, with the defensive man very close to the shooter. It is a grave error for any basketball player to simply walk on the court, even though he is the only player there, and leisurely shoot the basketball at the basket with any kind of shot.

We like to have our players stress quickness. If they are by themselves we want them to pitch the ball out with some backspin on it, run and retrieve it if it bounces from the floor, shoot the ball quickly, rebound it quickly; come back to their position, throw the ball to themselves again, go and get it and shoot, and so on. Any drill that stresses quickness is going to help any player improve his basketball shooting accuracy.

In teaching a boy to shoot a driving layup, we want the boy to move with great speed, either dribbling the ball, or without the ball, and receive a pass. Then he goes to position, where he jumps just as high as he can, not as far as he can, carries the ball up high with both hands, and then releases it either with his right hand if he is coming from the right side of the basket, or his left hand if he is coming from the left side of the basket. We stress carrying the ball with both hands and releasing it at the highest point with either one or the other.

In teaching a hook shot to our centers, again we stress control of the ball. We want our players, if they are shooting a right handed hook shot, to turn to their left, pick a spot on the board they wish to hit, carry the ball up high with both hands, and release it at the top of their jump, facing the basket, with their right hand. The same fundamentals apply, of course, if our pivot men are moving to their right and going to release a left handed hook shot.

The mental side of shooting is an equally important factor. We want our shooters to have a great deal of confidence in their shooting ability, to shoot without fear of missing; consequently we do not want any mental tensions affecting their shooting. We feel it is most important that our players be physically and mentally set to shoot the basketball, and try to help them arrive at the proper frame of mind.

We stress that shooting is a serious business and carelessness can never become a factor in one's shooting. We demand that our players, whether they be guards, forwards, or centers, practice shooting the type of shot that they will get from our offensive pattern. We want them to practice these shots and practice them profusely. We want them to develop a great deal of confidence in their own shooting, and our coaches aid in every possible way, not only in developing the physical side of shooting, but also the mental confidence of a shooter.

This can be done, of course, by working with these young men before, after, or during practice, praising their great effort and trying to correct any physical weakness which might be apparent. We feel that our team offense, both man to man and against a zone, does give all five of the players an opportunity to attempt to shoot. Consequently, our cardinal rule with our players is to shoot the basketball anytime the offense releases it for a shot, and to shoot only the shot they have practiced profusely.

We try to emphasize strongly that when a player goes up to shoot he must be absolutely sure in his own mind that he is going to make the basket. If the player develops this type of confidence, it will, beyond any shadow of a doubt, improve his shooting ability.

There are some other shooting rules which might be beneficial to the reader. We want our players, when they first come to practice, to shoot the ball quickly, as I have mentioned before, but to begin shooting the ball close to the basket and then retreat to their maximum range. We do not like any of our players to practice shooting the ball beyond a 22 or 25 foot distance from the basket, for our offense is geared to release our team for a shot from what we like to call the 20 foot distance. We like to have each player have a basketball at his disposal so that he can work by himself for a minimum of ten minutes a day just perfecting his shot.

If we have two boys on the basketball, we like to have one rebound and pass the ball back to the shooter, who shoots the ball, moves quickly to another spot, receives the ball from the rebounder, shoots again, moves quickly to still another spot and continues on until ten to twelve shots have been taken. Then the shooter and rebounder change places.

We also like to have, when we practice these two man shooting propositions, guard shoot with guard, center shoot with center, and corner men shoot with corner men. We want every minute of time on the basketball floor to be used to the player's advantage. If it is used to their individual advantage, of course, then it will be used to our team's advantage.

Summarizing our shooting drills and fundamentals, I would say that we stress quickness, concentration, proper holding and release of the ball, proper hand, arm, and eye coordination. We emphasize that shooting is a serious business and should be taken very seriously by every one of our players.

As a coach I follow the procedure of trying to change a shooter only if he is inaccurate in the manner in which he shoots the basketball. At the University of Michigan I have had the opportunity of coaching some very great players with unorthodox shooting styles. John Tidwell, who captained the 1961 Michigan team and who was one of the nation's great shooters, was a very unorthodox shooter. Although he violated a number of the fundamentals in which I believe, his shooting accuracy was such that I did not think I could improve it by changing his shot. At the collegiate level we only change a boy's shot if we feel we can improve his shooting accuracy.

I have also worked with beginning players, boys of the 10 to 13 year bracket, and in teaching them we do stress the fundamentals which have been discussed previously. There is no sure way to teach a boy to become a great shooter. Great shooters have been, almost without exception, players who (1) had a deep and enduring love of the game of basketball, and (2) were willing to expend monumental amounts of time in order to improve their basketball skills. Shooting is perhaps the most important of these skills.

As statistics show, shooting accuracy has been increasing on all levels, almost year by year. All of the amateur teams, high schools, junior high schools, and collegiate ball clubs have continually increased shooting percentages as the years progress. Where this might stop, I have no way of knowing; but in my honest opinion these percentages will continue to increase.

A young man, in order to become successful in basketball or any sport, must be willing to make many sacrifices. I would say that to become a great shooter a young man must be willing to spend an endless amount of time in just shooting the ball. In my judgment, good shooters are not born, but can be developed if the individual involved is willing to make the necessary sacrifices.

A. Rules to follow.
  1. Concentrate.
  2. Eye on basket (insures follow through).
  3. No carelessness.
  4. Full fingered shot—ball may rest on butt of hand, but fingertips control accuracy of shot.

Lay-in Drills—Two Line—Two Ball. We start C and D with balls under the basket. Line A, first man, drives for goal without the ball, receives pass from D, and shoots, right hand lay-in. As he shoots, the second man in line follows and receives pass from C and shoots. Line B men rebound each shot and pass to the next man in line. Two balls are kept in motion and everyone moves. Line A shooters run to the end of Line B. Line B rebounders go to the end of Line A. We discourage dribbling. We make Line B run for rebound and climb the board for it. Timing must be stressed. We run five drive-ins from this:

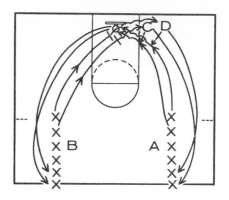

1. Right.
2. Left.
3. Middle.
4. Curl in front right.
5. Curl in front left.

We demand every shot to be the same, and allow no deviation from our prescribed shots. This drill must be run at top speed.

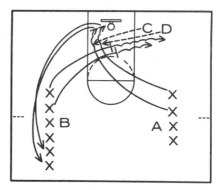

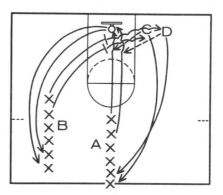

5. Stress quickness (two boys on ball or bounce ball to self).
6. Take ball up with both hands on jump shot.
7. Elbows should be in.
8. Start in close and move back to maximum range.
9. High jump on drive to basket—don't broad jump.

B. Psychological conditions of shooting—negative thinking (fear, anger, lack of confidence, worry) will affect shooting.

C. Physiological aspects of shooting—good shooters are consistent shooters and well conditioned boys are consistent.

D. Coaching principles in teaching shooting.
  1. The coach may demonstrate the proper techniques of shooting, hand position, elbow and arm, and so on, but the coach does not gain anything by shooting at the basket. No one can score with every shot, so do not try.
  2. The coach can make sure the boy is fundamentally sound, but only the boy himself can develop *touch* through constant and diligent practice.

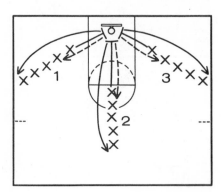

Three Line—Jump Shot Drill. Divide the team into three areas, as shown by X1, X2, and X3 lines. Start on command and first man in each line jump shoots, rebounds his own shot, and passes (sharply) back to next man in line. When one line scores 10 or 15, the lines are changed so that each line shoots from every spot.

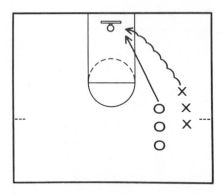

Pressure Shots—Drive-ins. We simply give offensive man X the ball and a three step lead on defense. On command whistle, he dribbles for the goal and O tries to beat him, stop his shot, and harass the shooter. This drill may be run from either side.

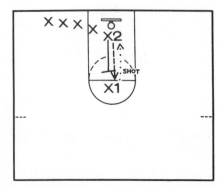

Jump Shots—Pressure. Line the team up under the basket with a shooter, X1, in high post area. Have X2 pass the ball to X1 and rush at him, trying to block X1's shot. X1 must shoot a jump shot and must shoot quickly.

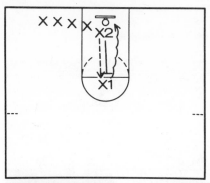

Drive Shots—Pressure. X2 passes to X1 and runs at him with his arms outstretched. X1 fakes a shot and drives for the goal, brushing X2 as he drives in a straight line for the basket. X1 must not circle around the charging X2 for the basket.

Larry Tregoning, Michigan. Right-hand layup.

Doug Herner, Michigan. Left-hand layup, driving.

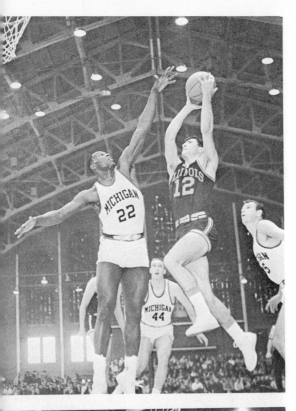

Tal Brodie, Illinois. Driving layup, left side of basket. Note Buntin of Michigan, inside hand defensive move.

Cazzie Russell, Michigan. Right-handed driving layup.

Cazzie Russell, Michigan. Right-hand lay-up, left side.

Cazzie Russell, Michigan. Right-handed stuff shot.

Cazzie Russell, Michigan. Right-handed jump shot.

Cazzie Russell, Michigan. Releasing a right-handed jump shot vs. Iowa.

Jim Myers, Michigan. Left-handed jump shot.

Bill Buntin, Michigan. Right-handed jump shot.

Bill Buntin, Michigan. Left-handed hook shot.

Bill Buntin, Michigan. Right-handed hook shot.

Bobby Cantrell, Michigan. Right-handed
jump shot.

George Pomey, Michigan. Right-handed
jump shot.

Gary Bradds, Ohio State. Bill Buntin, Michigan, defending.

Free Throw Shooting

There is not a basketball coach in the country who does not appreciate the importance of accurate free throw shooting. There is also not a basketball coach in the country, including myself, who would not give his right arm to learn better techniques for improving the foul shooting of the members of his team.

The foul shot is different from the normal shot in basketball, for this is one time when quickness in shooting is a hindrance rather than a help. This is the only time during the basketball game that the player may take his time (he has ten seconds from the time the ball is placed in his hands by the referee) and when no opposing player can in any way try to hinder his shot.

We try to introduce the following circumstances in teaching our boys to be accurate, high percentage foul shooters.

1. We want an element of fatigue in our players when they practice foul shots. Basketball is fatiguing, and rarely is the player fresh when he makes a foul or any other kind of shot.
2. We try to create an element of pressure on the boy practicing his foul shots. During the foul shooting situation, the spotlight is on the shooter, and he has to respond to the challenge immediately and without any help.

We utilize the following drills in competitive games in order to accomplish our purpose of creating pressure.

1. We divide our squad into two groups—the yellow and the blue. We start arbitrarily at one end of the court with seven or eight players on each team. They line up in a normal free throw situation; if the blue team has the ball, each blue player is allowed to shoot two foul shots. They retain possession of the ball as long as they score. If they miss, a rebounding situation goes into effect, and if the yellow team rebounds the ball they must advance it to mid-court, at which time they are allowed to go to the foul line and shoot individually. If the blue team gets the rebound they are allowed to continue shooting free throws. This puts an element of pressure on each player to do his job in shooting, rebounding, moving the ball up the court, and defending. We usually play this game to 40 points.

2. We conclude many practice sessions by making each boy hit an arbitrary number of fouls in succession. This can be four, six, or any number the coach decides. Remember, whatever decision or number may be reached, be sure that each boy has the ability to make it. Don't relax the rule or number once you have decided on it.

3. We divide our squad, with a team at each end of the court, and again give an arbitrary number of foul shots the team must make in succession before they can leave the court. This is higher than the number the individual must make, and since most boys are ready to leave practice at the conclusion of a grueling session, this puts pressure on each boy to carry his load and not miss. This is what we are striving for.

4. As mentioned previously, we start many game scrimmage situations with foul shooting, which has an actual effect on the situation itself. I have mentioned this work in describing our basketball plans, and we have found that it is an excellent way to test a boy's ability to respond to pressure and fatigue.

There are many ways of practicing this crucial part of basketball shooting. The coach cannot allow his foul shooting to become a rote process, but must try to simulate conditions under which these fouls would be shot in a normal game.

Our individual foul shooting techniques are the same as described in our section on shooting fundamentals. The basic difference, again, is that this shot need not be hurried.

We demand complete concentration and do everything in our power to aid the shooter's confidence in his ability to make every shot. We do not want to leave anything to chance, and want each boy fully prepared in this important shooting fundamental to respond to any clutch situation with a firm and positive attitude.

4

Offensive Basketball

Whereas defensive basketball is intensity, fierceness, aggressiveness, and controlled frenzy, offensive basketball is poise, patience, precision, definite plans, and the ability to meet any situation with well executed moves. Wishful thinking and "hope" shots only tend to make any defense look great.

Basketball is a team game. It is my considered opinion that the good offensive man is one who moves well *without* the ball. Consequently, a good offense in basketball is one in which all five members are moving. A sound offense has no place in it for the man who stands still. Keep moving in a prearranged plan. This will keep the defense moving and will not allow a defensive man to leave his man and cause trouble elsewhere. Alertness, of course, is all-important in offense basketball. No good offensive team, however, can be stereotyped to such an extent that individual moves and individual effort become mechanical. The well drilled, poised, offensive player will take the initiative and do what must be done in order to get the job done.

As a general rule, it is my contention that a shot may be taken by any player at any time—if it is a shot the boy has practiced and practiced profusely. It is also a cardinal rule that the ball should be controlled until such a shot presents itself to a player, regardless of the time factor. It might come after ten seconds of playing time, or after two minutes. Patience is certainly a virtue in offensive basketball. A set offense should be geared to accomplish the following things:

1. Release a boy for a good shot, preferably at less than 20 feet.
2. When the shot is taken, the floor must be balanced by the offense, in order to accomplish two things:
   a. Adequate offensive backboard coverage.
   b. Sufficient men in position to guard against a fast break.

A forced shot or pass is something which cannot be tolerated. When you have the ball, it is unnecessary to make this kind of play. A team skilled in fundamentals and mentally prepared to meet all situations will make a minimum amount of mistakes. No team can afford the luxury of relinquishing the ball without a shot and, in the vast majority of cases, the team which makes the fewest errors will win the ball game. A team that operates on this premise will be *successful*. Selfishness cannot be present in any one or any group of players if success is to be achieved.

A successful team operation provides satisfaction to every individual on the squad. A team with balanced scoring is a difficult team to combat defensively. Balanced scoring depends on personnel. The offense should provide an opportunity for all players to share in the scoring. Naturally, the more prolific the shooter, the more he will score. Remember the basic rule on shooting—shoot any time you have a shot that you have practiced. The only time this might not apply would be when you are stalling to accomplish a specific end.

On the following pages are the offensive maneuvers which have been used by our teams at the University of Michigan. I feel confident that this offense will enable us to handle any defensive alignment with which the opposition can confront us.

The coach's primary and fundamental duty is to prepare his team for every eventuality which may confront them on the basketball floor. Nothing can be left to hope or chance! As of this writing, I feel that the offense we use is the *best* one in operation today. We do plan to continue to improve, modify, change for the better, if necessary, all phases of our basketball, both offensive and defensive. Let me reiterate—the coach who stands "pat" is a dead man!

BASIC FORMATION VS. ANY TYPE OF DEFENSE

Description of formation. Basically, this is a two out three in offensive formation and we place our men in normal conventional spots, as follows:

X5—post man. We like to start him high primarily to give our guard with the ball three outlet passes, i.e., other guard, strong side forward, and high post man. As will be shown, we have a definite offensive move planned when the guard does hit the high post man. He will start low if he feels that the guards need an opening to drive down middle or as a change of pace.

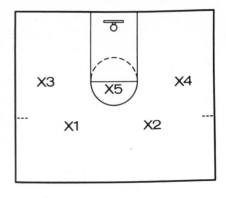

X3 and X4—corner men. Position selves at foul line extended and five to seven feet from sideline. Must not be forced closer to side as guard must have room to go outside.

X1 and X2—guards. Split width difference between post and corner men and line up approximately ten feet in front of foul line.

GUARD OUTSIDE SERIES: SWING TIGHT (EITHER SIDE)

This offense is our basic one. We have found that it (if worked correctly) is very profitable, as far as balanced scoring is concerned. Many will notice, and correctly, that the reverse action is the keynote of this offense. For our purposes, keeping the post man, X5, tight to foul line and moving high to foul line after weak side forward has cleared has been very successful.

Our diagrams show everything starting to the right, but we do emphasize a balanced start, half right and half to left. This is the only way this offense can be effective. If we do not get a shot at the conclusion of our moves (Diagram 4), we then square up, regroup in our original positions, and our guards begin a new offensive thrust.

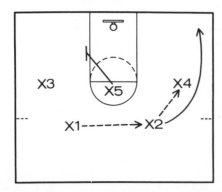

Diagram 1. X1 passes to X2 to make defense move. X2 passes to X4, runs hard to outside to corner, being alert for handoff as he passes, X4 pivots with ball toward scoring area. When X5 sees X2 hit X4 and move outside, X5 moves to position approximately seven feet from basket on weak side of floor. X5 faces ball, X4, and sets screen.

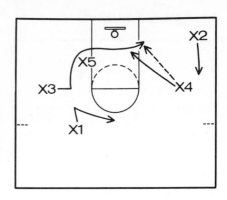

Diagram 2. X3 moves across keyhole area to strong side, using X5 as post, 60 per cent low and 40 per cent high. X3 must fake one way and go the other to confuse defense. X4, with ball, passes to X3 if he is open and follows pass to cover board. X3 shoots. When X4 passes ball, X2 reverses to take up defensive spot.

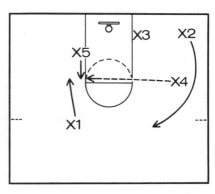

Diagram 3. If X4 does not hit X3, who has moved across (per Diagram 2), he looks for X5—who, as X3 moves by him, steps to high post position at foul line and looks for cross court pass. When X4 hits X5, X5 may shoot short jump shot, drive for goal, or hand ball to X1, who drives for goal when cross court pass is thrown.

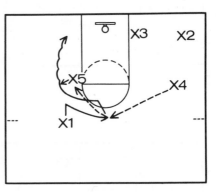

Diagram 4. If X4 does not hit X3, first option or X5, second option, he may hit X1, weak side guard, with the ball. X1 has faked in and receives ball at a position midway between the foul lines. X1 then hits X5 at a choke post position and moves off him in a two on two basketball move, going outside or down the middle, trying to get defense to commit an error.

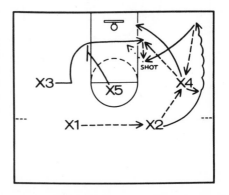

Diagram 5. If, as suggested in Diagram 1, X4 hands to X2, X2 goes to corner and passes back to X4, who hits X3 and follows his pass. X2 scissors off X4 back, receives ball on double cut from X3, and shoots. We use this handoff and scissor from the corner to keep the defense honest.

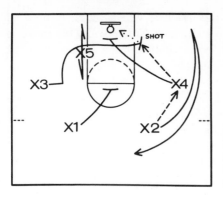

Backboard Coverage for Diagram 2. X5 takes left corner of board; X3 (shooter) takes right corner; X4 takes middle; X1 takes high post; X2 runs back for deep safety.

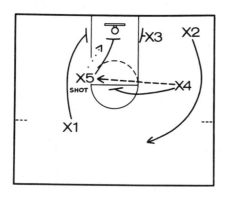

Backboard Coverage for Diagram 3. X5 (shooter) follows and takes middle; X3 has right side; X4 takes high post; X1, who breaks for goal, covers left side; X2 retreats as safety man.

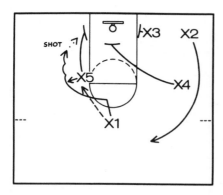

Backboard Coverage for Diagram 4. In this weak side post move, X5 takes left side of board; X4 takes center; X3 takes right; X2 deep safety; X1 fights back for high post spot after shot.

One last important variation in this offense, which again is used to keep the defense honest, is what we call our *GO* move. This move is very effective against teams which are switching their defensive front line and using their defensive center to pick up our swing man or weak side forward.

This *GO* move is simply executed. The only cue is that the weak side forward, X3 in our diagrams, comes up behind X5 and does not cut by him but shouts a verbal *GO* and slaps X5 on the rump. X5 moves across key and X3 becomes post man and moves high and tight.

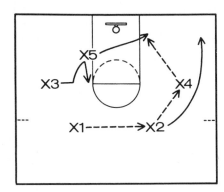

Go Move. This is simply a move where X3 weak side forward and X5, on given verbal signal GO and physical slap, exchange positions and offensive responsibilities.

GUARD THROUGH SERIES: CLEAR

This series is designed as a supplement and a complement to our swing tight series. No signal is needed. This move is keyed when the strong side guard hits forward and clears to goal.

It has been our experience that this move against man to man defenses will invariably result in a short 15 to 17 foot jump shot for the weak side guard. Also, we have found that we can always pass the ball from the strong side forward, X4, to the post man, X5, as he moves off the tail of the through guard. This move does get the ball to your post man 15 feet from the basket. He can maneuver for shot, particularly if the post man's defensive man picks up the weak side guard. Actually, the weak side guard can drive all the way for the goal.

Remember—it is important for the through guard to run hard for the goal, looking for ball and clear out to his defensive spot. This is a good move for a sharp shooting guard.

We will run this move equally right and left. This clear move develops in a hurry. We call it or run it when we need an immediate 15 foot shot, i.e., late in game, right before half, and so on. We call this one of our "bread and butter" moves.

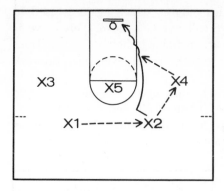

Diagram 1. X1 passes to X2. X2 passes to X4, steps to inside, and moves hard for goal—looking for a return pass from X4. X2's hands are in position to receive pass. If he does, he goes for goal and scores.

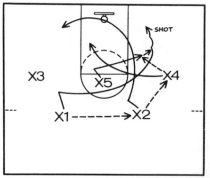

Diagram 2. As X2 clears toward goal, X5 comes off his tail to a strong side post position. X4 passes to X5 and cuts hard to a high post position. X1 fakes left, comes hard off X4, receives pass from X5, and goes to score.

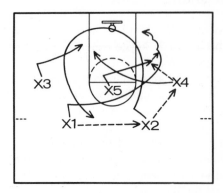

Diagram 3. X2 must move through and to goal and he must move with speed. X2 must clear and circle out as he becomes the safety valve defensively.

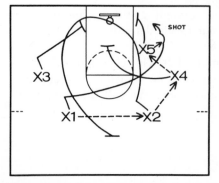

Diagram 4. Board coverage: X4 has center responsibility; X5 has right side; X3 has left side; X1 short post; X2 deep responsibility.

SPECIAL SCORING PLAYS

Forward

Blue (Verbal Call). X2 hits X4 and he and X1 exchange positions. X5 moves to base line approximately 12 feet from basket on strong side. X4 hits X5 and moves across keyhole looking for return pass. X3 comes across hard and smashes his man into X4 and his defensive man, X3, moves to base line and may receive ball for 15 foot jump shot. X5 may fake to X3 and wheel for shot himself. X4 covers weak side of board; X5 wheels to middle after passing off; X3 has right side; X2 takes high post; X1 stays deep.

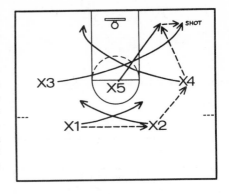

Green (Verbal Call). X2 hits X4 and goes hard outside, as in the swing move. X4 returns ball at once to X1. X1 hits X3 at once. X3 tries to hit X4 who has come off the double pick, which was formed by X2 coming out of corner and X5, who comes from high post to join X2 in forming this pick. Option is for X5 to peel back to high post after X4 has cleared. This will free X5 if his man switches to pick up X4. X4's man is invariably picked by the two offensive screeners, X2 and X5.

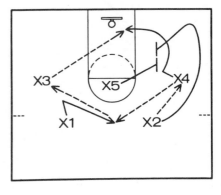

Guard Scoring

Weak Side Series (Set). X2 hits X4 and stands still—key to set weak side. X4 returns ball to X2 and heads across high post area looking for ball and clearing side. X5 fakes to base line when he sees what's up and then comes back to high post off X4's tail. X2 hits X1, and X1 hits X5. X2 breaks hard for goal and returns pass from X5. If he is open, he has a layup. Option—if X2 (when he breaks) is covered by his defensive man, he cuts in front of high post and X1 double cuts off him. The success of this play is dependent on X4's defensive man not alerting X2's defensive man that he was unprotected in rear. It is also predicated on the fact that in the majority of cases X2's defensive man will watch the ball as X2 passes to X1, thereby allowing X2 to beat him with a straight cut.

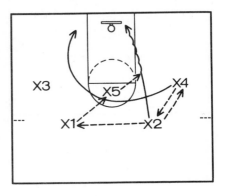

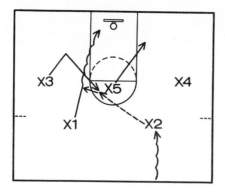

Weak Side Series (Quick). Our strong side guard X2 hits weak side forward X3 at high post position. X3 breaks to this position and that keys the play. As X2 hits X3, the weak side guard X1 breaks for goal. X3 hits X1 if he is open, or X3 may turn and shoot as he is 15 feet from goal. This move is effective if the defensive guards are pressuring the offensive guards.

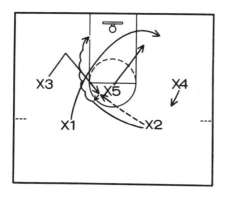

Weak Side Series (Quick Trailer). We run this maneuver regardless of the pressure, but if there is no defensive pressure, we then run X2 as a trailing guard featuring X2 in this offensive thrust.

Guard to High Post

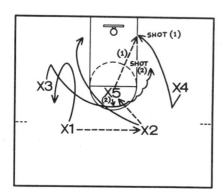

Popeye. X1 hits X2, guard to guard. X2 fakes to X4 and hits X5 at high post and follows pass. X1 joins X2 and forms a double screen for X3 who heads for top of circle. X4 back cuts at the moment that X2 fakes to him and hits X5. X5's first option is to hit X4. X5's second option is to hit X3 at the top of circle. X3 may drive for basket as X4's side is clear or he, X3, may shoot from on top.

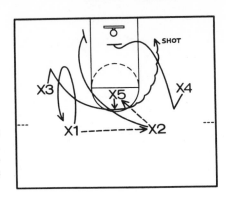

Popeye. X1 and X2 go in side by side and X1 peels off and gets back on defense. X2 covers corner of board. X4 covers center of board. X3, if drive is to right, covers right corner. X5 also smashes board.

Popeye is an excellent maneuver to use against defensive corner men who are putting great pressure on the strong side offensive forward. As shown, this maneuver ensures the strong side forward, X4 in this case, the perfect back cut opportunity.

The forwards must be drilled in this back cut routine and much time must be spent with the post man perfecting this drop pass to the back cutting corner men. When perfected, this can be an excellent offensive move. Popeye is automatic any time the guard rams the ball to the high post man.

In the 1964-65 season we modified slightly our Popeye move and used the following split in addition to the double pick.

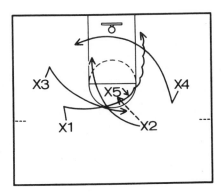

Rather than X1 and X2 setting a double pick for the weak side corner man, X3, they now split the high post. X4's back cut and X3's move to the top are exactly as they were in the double pick Popeye move.

MICHIGAN'S 1-3-1 ATTACK

Strong (Smash)

This offensive move was designed to take advantage of the great offensive potential of Cazzie Russell, Michigan's great All-American guard. We feel, however, that this strong move can be effective regardless of the guard personnel. Like any other offense, the better the players, the more effective the offense.

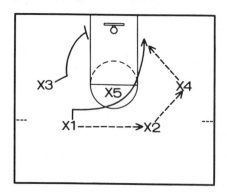

X1 hits X2 and X2 hits X4. XI moves fast for goal, trying to brush his man off X5. X4 tries first to hit X1 at the low post and X1 shoots. X3 moves in to cover the weak side corner of the backboard.

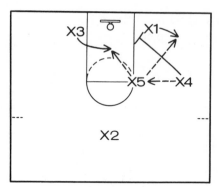

If X4 cannot hit X1 at the low post, he looks next to hit X5, who has moved to the strong side of the high post. If X4 passes to X5, he then (X4) *smashes* for the hoop. X1 takes advantage of the screen and moves out approximately 15 feet from the basket, looks to receive the ball from X5, and takes his shot. When X5 gets the ball he can either hit X1, turn and shoot, or hit X3, who fights for a position at the low post in the three second area.

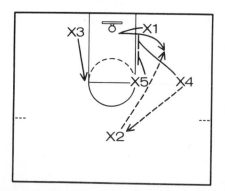

If X4 cannot hit either X1, low post, or X5, he passes out to X2 and smashes for the hoop. X5 also goes for the base line. X1 moves under the basket when he sees the pass thrown to X2 and then reverses quickly and takes advantage of a double pick by X4 and X5.

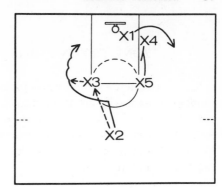

X2 may pass to X1, who takes a 15 foot jump shot, or he can hit X3, who has moved to a "choke" post position, and X2 and X3 can play two on two basketball.

Number (Verbal Call)

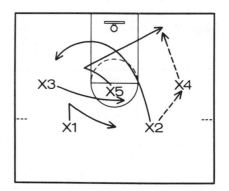

X2 hits X4 and heads for goal. X5, upon hearing number, steps back to weak side low post and breaks off X2 as he comes through. X4 hits X5, if possible. X3 heads for high post and looks for ball.

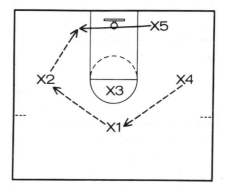

If X4 cannot hit X5, we want a *quick reverse*, a pass to X1, who hits X2, and X5 reverses quickly on the base line to the strong side. X2 hits him with the ball and he, X5, shoots.

This move (similar to our low zone move) was put in to utilize the scoring prowess of our center. We found it to be a very effective offensive weapon. We would test any defense at the outset of a game with this maneuver. We know at once, by sending guard through, if defense is man to man or zone. This play is cued by our guard calling any number (1-2-3, and so on), or just calling the word "number."

ZONE OFFENSE AGAINST EVEN MAN OUT

The zone offense which we deploy against a zone is predicated on the number of men who are in the attacking line of their zone. We attack an even front line, such as a 2-3 zone or 2-1-2 zone, with an odd man out. Actually, both of the zone offenses end up attacking as a 1-3-1 offense. We call these offenses high or low, and these positions designate the position of our post man.

High Zone Offense vs. 2-3 or 2-1-2 Zone

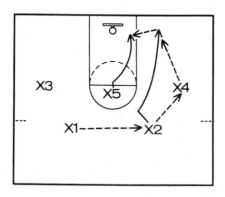

X1 hits X2. Guard to guard. X2 hits X4 and steps in and then moves to base line, making sure he goes behind the defensive man who will challenge X4. X4 looks to base line and hits him, if possible. If X4 hits X2, then X5 drives for goal. X2 shoots or hits X5.

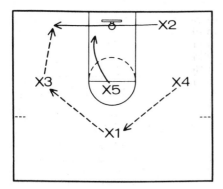

If X4 cannot hit X2, then he reverses ball to X1, who reverses quickly to X3. X2 roams base line to strong side and X3 hits him, if possible. X5 drives for goal any time the ball is passed to base line man. Theory is (and this is an actuality) that the middle man of the zone will have to cover base line man, thereby freeing X5 or the offensive post man. If, after X2 roams base line one time, he does not receive ball, then he returns to the guard position and X1 hits forward and penetrates, and the same series and sequences are started again.

Low Zone Offense
vs. 2-3 or 2-1-2

1. Post man on base line.
2. Run either side.

X1 hits X2, and X2 hits X4 and goes hard for goal. X5 starts on base line and moves to strong side, and X3 goes hard for high post looking for ball. X5 positions self approximately 12 to 15 feet from basket on strong side. X4, with ball, looks to base line man X5, hits him if possible, and then to high post area X3. X2 replaces X3 as weak side wing man.

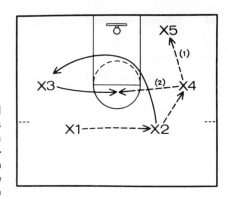

If X4 hits X5, X3 moves for goal. If X4 cannot hit either X5 on base line or high post man, the ball is passed back to point at X1 and then into X2. X5 then moves across base line to strong side. This is the quick reverse. We stay with this until a shot is taken and then we smash backboard hard.

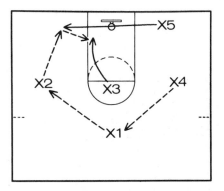

The primary principle in these zone offenses attacking an even number out 2-3 or 2-1-2 is to move into a 1-3-1 attack with post man at high post (HIGH) or on base line (LOW). Remember, whenever a pass is made to base line man, the man at high post breaks for goal.

Zone Offense vs. Odd Man Out 1-3-1 or 1-2-2 Zone

This is what we call our position zone offense, and it is predicated on positioning our men at proper spots to take advantage of the weaknesses which are inherent in this zone.

We merely try to move the ball to the nearest outlet man, and we depend on hitting the 15 foot shot. Our rule is the same in that our post man must go for goal when the ball is passed into base line. Also, when our high post man, X5, receives ball, he looks for base line cutters X3 or X4.

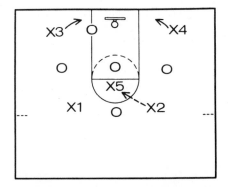

63

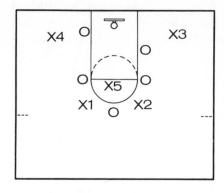

We also run this against a 1-2-2, again looking for good ball handling to make the defense move. We look for the easy jump shot or lay-in.

Even against these defenses, we have had success in running zone offenses which put us in the 1-3-1 offenses. We do start, however, with the position zone offenses which we call POINT.

In attacking any zone, we operate under the following rules:

1. We play with patience, poise, and a knowledge of what we are doing.
2. If we are zoned, we figure that the opposition is a weak defensive club or that they are trying to surprise us. (As we work against a zone prior to every game, we cannot be surprised.)
3. We know we can hurt a team zoning us on our offensive board for, even though they always have men in rebounding position, they do not screen our men out, as no defensive man has a definite assignment.
4. We emphasize speed in our attack to beat their zone back.
5. We emphasize again our basic offensive rules—our plans are based on five men operating with patience and poise and with the knowledge that what we are striving to accomplish has been successful and will be again. We like to think that our team plays with great confidence regardless of the defense.

The zone defense has a place in basketball, in my judgment. However, I feel that some coaches, and the teams which reflect their opinion, have an unrealistic fear of a zone. I firmly believe in the following statements and have been successful in convincing my team of these facts:

1. A zone defense can only hurt us if it surprises us. Since we work every week against this defense, we cannot be caught short.
2. A zone cannot replace or be better than a man to man defense. If a team plays a weak man to man defense, or plays only zone, then that defense has defects.
3. A zone does not provide for adequate defensive board coverage. The men under the basket do not have men and therefore do not try to pick them off

the defensive board. Our team is convinced we can kill the zone of our offensive board if everyone goes to the board.

4. The zone defense is more effective when combined with man to man principles. This type of defense is used by the University of Tennessee. Also the zone trap defense, which consists of trapping the ball with two or more men, is effective. The University of Kentucky used this 1-3-1 trap zone effectively.

DELAY TO SCORE OFFENSE

Placement of players. X2 is our best move with and without the ball. The object is to isolate him 1 on 1 with his defensive man. X5 is moved out of the moving part of the maneuver. He is a safety man. He is the post man and he takes their post man off the board. X1, X3, and X4 are in the rotation, and form a triangular rotation.

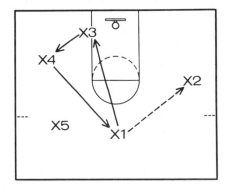

Moves. X1 hits X2, cuts for goal, looks for pass, and then takes X3's spot. X4 replaces X1 and looks for pass from X2. X2 should hit X4 as he moves for X1's position. If X4 is covered he does not wait for the pass but cuts for the basket without the ball and back cuts his man. X3 replaces X4.

Theory. X2 may beat his man anytime, with or without the ball, and score a layup. We are in this offense to score, although the nature of it causes a delay. The secret of success is your X2 man. He must be a confident, sure ball handler, as he will determine the effectiveness of this offense. We use this offense when we are ahead, usually in the latter stages of the game—in that grey area when we feel it is too early to use a dead stall, but too late to just continue our offense and possibly give up the ball.

The following examples will illustrate when we used this offense, once when it helped us win a most important game and once when we gave up the ball while using it, and hence lost the game.

We were playing the defending national champions, Loyola of Chicago, in Minneapolis, Minnesota, in the opening round of the 1964 Mid East Regional Championships. With approximately five minutes to go we had a nine point lead, but lost six points of this lead in two and one-half minutes because of Loyola's great full court defensive pressure game. With almost three minutes to play and the momentum all Loyola's, we went into this drive offense. Larry Tregoning, our forward, moved out from X4's position, received a pass from Russell, returned the ball to

Russell, cut by his man, received the return pass, and scored a layup. We went on to win this game by three points. This was, in my judgment, the key basket of the game.

We lost to Wisconsin in Ann Arbor by using this offense in the following manner. I do not blame this offense, or any player, as this was just a missed shot.

We set up this drive offense in order to isolate our center under the basket. Therefore, our post man was X1 in this maneuver. We had him hit X2, break for the basket and then, instead of following the line of

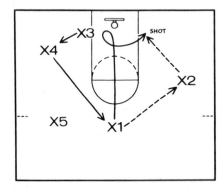

Drive with Option.

movement of X3, he hooked back to a strong side position at the low post, received a pass, and unfortunately missed a relatively easy shot. There were a couple of minutes to go, and we led by three, but they recovered the ball, scored, and went on to win. This play perhaps did not lose the game, but I felt that, had we scored, we would have won.

STALL OFFENSE

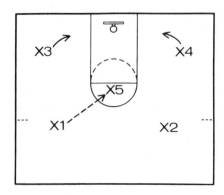

Spot. When we discover the defensive team is in any type of zone press defense, we spread our offense and move the ball. No dribbling or moving men are necessary if the ball is handled properly. We try to hit the high post, and then he turns and looks for X3 and X4 moving for basket. We will score on this, layups only.

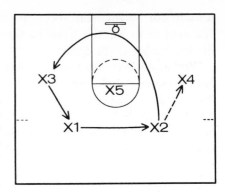

Rotate—Guard to Forward. Against man to man press, we move our men in the following manner: Guard to forward X2 hits X4 and moves for goal and replaces X3. X1 replaces X2, X3 replaces X1. X4 with ball may hit X2 cutting for goal, X5 at high post, or X1, who moves for X2's spot.

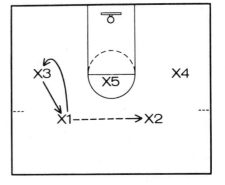

Guard to Guard vs. Man to Man Press. X1 hits X2. X1 and X3 exchange positions. X2 may hit X4, and our guard to forward move is automatic. X2 may hit X5. If so, we remain stationary. X2 may hit X3, who has replaced X1 at the guard spot, and we are in our guard to guard move with X2 and X4 changing positions.

During the 1965-66 season we changed our stall offense to the one described. We did this in order to eliminate, or try to eliminate, the cross court pass, and also to get the ball to our best and surest basketball player. This stall never backfired on us, and I feel that it has a little more merit than our rotation one, although both have good points.

One of the most (if not the most) difficult decisions a coach must make is when to go into a stall game. There is no easy answer, but once we made the decision to stall we used this offense and instructed our team to shoot layups only.

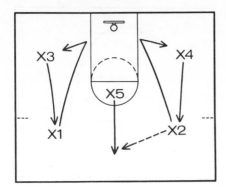

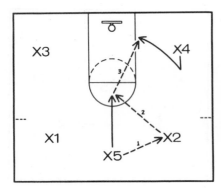

We spread our offensive men more than normal and place our best player (in 1965-66, Cazzie Russell) at the high post. This player, X5, is the key and must free himself all the time if this is to work. This stall can be used only against a pressure man to man, so of course your club must be ahead, with time running out. X5's area is from the center circle to the basket. X1, X2, X3, and X4's general movement areas are shown, except any player in the corner may back cut at any time X5 has the ball. If X2 hits X5 high, both sides interchange. This keeps everyone moving and X2, the passer, can often run by his man, receive a return pass, and score.

This movement, from X1 or X2 to X5 and then the interchange, is pretty much the stall pattern. X5 must move quickly, and if he is overplayed he can back cut his man for easy baskets. If the pass goes from X2 to X4 or to X1 to X3, i.e., guard to corner man, then X5 cuts hard for the goal and looks for the return pass. This is effective, as the opposing team realizes X5 is the key and they try, or should try, to cut off X5. If they are successful, your stall is destroyed.

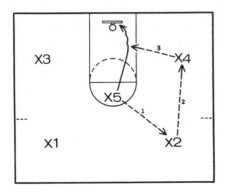

In my judgment, there is no real patterned way to stall to perfection. Your team must be ready, conditioned, and poised to stall, and to prepare them takes patience, time, and effort on the coach's part. This game is played when both teams are fatigued and your stall is effective if your club is more ready, both physically and mentally, than the opposition. The offensive stalling team should have the advantage, since it has the lead and the ball.

My basic thought on stalling is, again, to have your team prepared to stall correctly and with confidence. This is the coach's job, so don't leave anything to chance. In the dying moments of the tough game your team, whether it be a few points ahead or behind, or tired, looks to the coach for help and leadership, and the coach had better be in a position to lead. This is not an easy time, with the great noise and drama being unfolded, but the winning coach is normally the one best prepared himself, and who has best prepared his team to handle the situation. I personally do not think that luck has a great deal to do with winning close games.

FAST BREAK

Basketball has become America's most popular spectator sport, because it is an action game—and the fast break has contributed a great deal to this action. As previously stated, we believe in the fast break as an integral part of our over-all offensive plan. I do not, however, believe that the fast break is necessarily our most important offensive weapon. In other words, we will never put all of our offensive eggs into the fast break basket, but we do want the break to be run effectively.

The fast break is based on certain sound fundamentals in basketball, and we practice diligently the manner in which we think the break should be run. The important points we stress in our practice and in developing the fast break are as follows:

1. All of the drills which we run in building an effective break are run at top speed. Speed is essential in capitalizing on the fast break, and this is stressed from the very beginning. In these drills, which demand speed and coordination, we discover which boys can maneuver best with the ball, and it is these boys we hope to feature as the middle man in our fast break.
2. We know that the fast break is made or stopped on our defensive backboard. Unless we are a team skilled in the fundamentals of rebounding and able to capture our share of defensive rebounds, it is senseless for us to feature the fast break. The success of our fast break depends upon how quickly we break from defense to offense and, in particular, how quickly our defensive corner-

men break from the defensive board. We work a great deal on our rebounding and on our outlet pass. We not only want the ball cleared from the defensive backboard quickly, but we have to get that outlet pass to our guard quickly and accurately. We strive to get the ball to the middle man just prior to mid-court, and we want him to take the ball by a dribble to the foul line. When the man with the ball reaches the foul line, we want him to stop. We never allow our middle man to pass this point. This man practices a great deal on stopping with the ball, faking, passing to a wing man, or shooting from this point. Even after this man in the middle has passed the ball to the wing man, we want him to remain stationary, in a position to accept a return pass, and be ready to shoot a 15 foot shot.

In all of our drills we never allow the ball to be passed more than two times once the man has reached the foul line with it. Under normal conditions, this is the maximum amount of time the offensive breakers will have and, therefore, they must trigger a shot after one or two passes. We discourage the cross-court pass, that is, a pass from wing man to wing man. We like to have the ball go from the middle man to the wing man, who either shoots the ball on a driving layup, or, if the defense recovers in time to stop him, shovels the ball back to the middle man, who shoots.

We want our boys running for the break to picture the court in three offensive lanes, each approximately 15 feet in width. The total width of the court is 50 feet. We like to have our boys filling the three lanes in order to spread the defense and make it difficult for one or two of their men to cover two or three men of ours. We want our team to run hard at all times in order to get into the break. Many times, if your team is skilled and well drilled in running for this break, they can actually run by the defenders, who are not hustling back on defense as quickly as they should, and therefore get into the break and score two points very quickly.

3. Prior to 1964, we used to stress running the break to its conclusion only if we had an offensive man advantage when our man with the basketball in the middle stopped at the foul line. By man advantage, I mean that we had either a three on two or two on one situation. However, we have now given our team the leeway to shoot the basketball, even if they are covered (for example, three on three), if the defense is in a transitional state and our offensive players find themselves open in the 15 foot shooting area. Many teams, in hustling back on the defense, will have us covered man for man, or we will not have a numerical advantage, but they will be in a transitional stage of their defense, each boy looking for his own man. In some instances, the defensive man will leave a particular player on our team in order to cover his own man, and consequently the player he has left will have an unencumbered shot. I think it's very important that the boys on your team know what the coach's thinking is on this particular point. We have done it both ways at the University of Michigan, and feel that the second way, which allows one of our players to shoot the ball when he knows he's in good position to score, regardless of the defensive alignment, is the most productive.

4. We expect all five of our players to run for the break, knowing that three of them will be the important people in it. We want our fifth man, who has the view of the court in his vision, to stop at mid-court in order to delay as a safety valve. One of the hazards of the fast break, of course, is going down on the break, shooting with a man advantage, missing or losing the ball to the opposition who whip it out quickly and, therefore, finding yourself defending against a break. Consequently, we want, as I stated, the fifth man to delay and react to the situation as it occurs. Our fourth man down is also a safety valve man. We do not crash this fourth man as a trailer, as we feel that by crashing this man to the offensive board along with our other three we are in a vulnerable position defensively, and that position is one we wish to avoid.

The fast break requires mastery of all the fundamentals. Effective rebounding is of the utmost importance because no team, regardless of its speed, can run without the basketball. Accurate passing with boys running at top speed is essential. Speed dribbling from mid-court to the foul line is important, and, of course, shooting the basketball, blazing under the board at top speed is a necessity. A coach cannot just make the statement that he will have a fast break basketball team. It requires hours and hours of diligent hard work: the players must know exactly what is expected of them, and the coach must know exactly what he wants from his basketball players and drill them in the proper way to deliver these demands.

We have a number of simple drills we use to emphasize fundamental things which we desire our team to do when they are breaking for the opponent's goal. The main drills we use are as follows:

1. We line our team at the base line on three lines. We just have these three lines move down the court, parallel with one another, passing the ball back and forth until the middle man gets to the foul line, where he passes to a wing man or stops and shoots. Even if he passes the ball, he stops. As previously stated, we have the middle man stop on every occasion, as he becomes a logical outlet man after he's passed the ball or has a 15 foot shot, a shot which we consider a good one.
2. We run a simple three man drill, pass and go behind, or figure eight drill down the court, base line to base line.
3. The third three man drill without any defense which we use is as follows: The coach shoots the ball with the idea of missing; the man in the middle rebounds it and hits the wing man quickly with an outlet pass; he then moves to the opposite wing. The weak side wing man heads immediately for the center of the court and receives the ball just prior to mid-court. After he receives the ball he dribbles as fast as he can for the foul line. The outlet pass man and the rebounder are the wing men, and they fill the outside lane and run hard for the basket. The middle man, when he reaches the foul line, may of course either hit the wing man or stop and shoot the ball.

4. We run what we call three on two both ways. We split our squad, with half the boys at each end of the court. We start three men on the attack with the basketball, and they are faced by two defenders at the opposite end of the court. The defense also has a third man on the wing who joins them when the ball is shot. When the defensive men gain possession of the ball they become the offense and attack the opposite goal. There are two defenders waiting there with the third man on the wing, and a continuity is thus set in motion. This is a continuing drill, with the coach stressing the fundamentals he desires. There can be no relaxing, no carelessness in the running of this or any drill. This drill may be run for as long as the coach desires.

5. We run what we think is an effective three on two drill, which is run just one way. We run this full court with two sets of defenders; each set of defenders consists of two men. Three offensive men rebound and the two defensive men break back to their defensive keyhole position from the top of the keyhole, where they would normally be playing defensive guard. We feel that this drills us in getting back quickly on the defense, getting quickly into our two man tandem defense, and also teaches the offense to attack with speed and agility.

After the basket has been made or the defense rebounded the ball, start another group of five toward the offensive basket. Make the five boys who have completed the drill run back to the beginning base line to start this drill again. This has to be an action drill. We run two on one drill in the same manner we run three on two drill.

6. We run what we consider a very effective fast break drill which combines both three on two and two on one principles. We utilize a full court, put two defenders at one end, and line up the rest of our team in three lanes facing them in the opposite end of the court. We then have the middle man rebound the ball, make the quick outlet pass, and go opposite; we begin our break in this manner. At the opposite end of the court, when the ball is at the foul line, the offense, of course, tries to score. If they score or if the defense rebounds a missed shot, the defensive men automatically become the offensive men and the middle man in the fast break has to retreat to the opposite end of the court. Consequently we have a two on one situation in operation. The two wing men remain at the basket that they originally attacked, and after the two on one break is completed three more offensive players attack the two wing men at the other end, who thus become the defenders. This is another fine, ball handling, speed drill which can be run just as long as the coach feels he is gaining any positive action from it.

We keep our fast break drills simple, and work very hard to have our players develop correct habits. I think it is very difficult to preposition your men defensively, if you're in a man to man, in the starting positions in the fast break. I say this because no one knows exactly where the offensive men they are guarding are going to be.

On a team basis, we spend a great deal of time on five on five, with the defensive team gaining possession of the ball only if they can steal it prior to a shot being taken, or if they can rebound it on a missed shot. If they rebound it we emphasize that they break just as quickly as possible for the opponent's goal. We do stress in this the outlet pass, filling the lanes quickly and the three men attacking as swiftly as they can toward the opponent's goal. I do not want to give the impression that we run wild and will shoot the ball even if we are covered at the opposite end of the court. We do allow our team to judge when the ball should be shot. We do not want it forced to the basket. If the defense is back and we are contained, our plan is to set up in our basic offensive patterns and run these patterns until one of our players frees himself for a good shot. Briefly, therefore, our theory on the break is to utilize it if we can, to our advantage, and try for the break each time. We want our club to attack quickly and, if the break occurs, take it. If not, we want them to use patience, set up in their offensive formation, and maneuver until they get a good shot.

One important last thought on the fast break is the conduct of two of our offensive players when they have a man advantage and are attacking two on one. We like to have the ball passed back and forth prior

Fast Break Drills

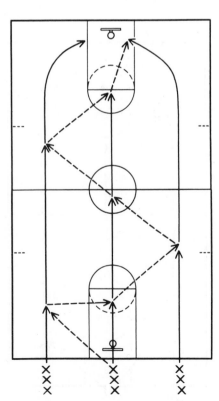

Parallel Lines.

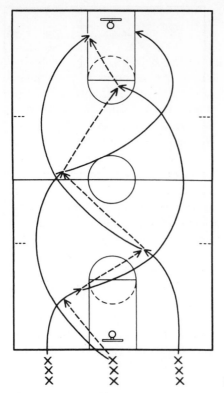

Pass and Follow Pass.

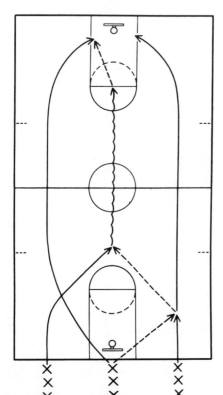

Pass and Go Away.

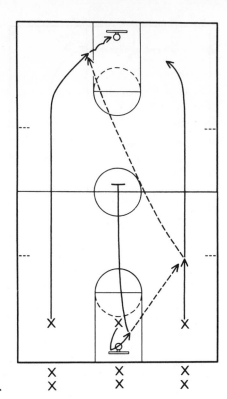

Pass and Pass to Long Cutter (Wing).

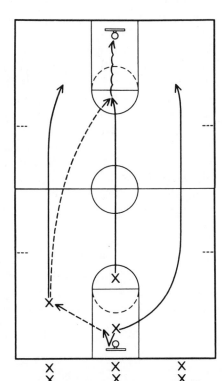

Pass and Pass to Long Cutter (Center).

to mid-court if this is feasible. Once the ball passes mid-court, however, we want one of our players to dribble very strongly for the basket so that by this offensive act the defensive man must commit himself. Once he's committed himself, either by taking the offensive man with the ball or by dropping back, our offensive man makes the proper move, which is either continuing for the basket with a layup or passing the ball to his teammate.

These drills provide our team with an opportunity to defend against the break. In any three on two drill we have two defenders, and these boys learn the proper way to defend against this particular situation. We teach them to play this in tandem, that is, one behind the other. The man in front attacks the ball which, in a proper situation, will be coming down the middle, and he makes this middle man stop and pass the ball either to one side or the other. In other words, our top man plays the ball one on one. The moment the ball is passed to the wing man the back man attacks the ball and plays the wing man one on one, while the middle man drops quickly back and guards the zone under the basket. If the ball is shot, we are in a position to rebound. If the ball goes back to the middle man, the man who is guarding the zone under the basket charges him as quickly as possible with his hand in the air, and the man who has been on the wing man one on one drops back under the basket. By this time help in the form of our defensive teammates should arrive.

In a two on one situation we want the defender to retreat. We have our man run backwards quickly, faking at the man with the ball, in the hopes that he will pull up. We tell our defensive men that if they can make the man with the ball pull up at least 15 feet from the basket, then they should leave him and allow him to take this shot. In other words, we want to avoid giving up the dead layup. We tell the defender that there will come a time when he will have to commit himself and take the man with the ball, and therefore to take him just as tough, mean, and ugly as he possibly can in order to discourage the very cheap basket. We want to avoid fouling, but we do want good action, shouting, motion, or anything to distract the shooter.

In addition to the three on two, both ways; two on one, both ways; and the three on two, two on one combination drills which have been described, we also like to run a three on three, both ways, drill.

We give three men the ball and they attack. When the other three men obtain possession of the ball, either by a steal, a rebound, or a made goal, they break. The offensive team becomes defensive and retreats to defend their goal. We like to play this for one round trip, then two, and then more. This is one of the best conditioning drills I know, and the coach can discover who is willing to punish himself in this drill. The laggard stands out like a sore thumb.

As another innovation, after the defensive team gains possession, make an offensive team member touch the base line before he can break to defense. This gives the breaking team an automatic man advantage, but they will have it for just a short time, so they must hurry. This drill teaches quickness and reaction under pressure.

As one can see, the drills that we use in order to build and maintain an effective fast break are simple drills; but again we feel they are very effective and in keeping with our philosophy of how the game of basketball should be played.

CHAPTER 5

Defensive Techniques

Any basketball team must have a sound defense. The only key to defensive success is the hard and strenuous work necessary for a player to become proficient defensively. A lapse, either physically or mentally, when playing the defense is always costly. *Never relax* on the defense is a cardinal rule. To be a sound defensive player, a boy must be alert, aggressive, and ambitious every second he is playing.

The most important job the basketball coach has today is selling his team on the value of defense. It is imperative for the success of the ball club that each player understands the sacrifice that is necessary for him to contribute defensively to the success of the team. Pride is the keynote. A team which takes great pride in its defense is difficult to beat.

Defense is work, practice, sweat, blood, collisions, mental and physical toughness; but, basically, any basketball player can excel defensively. It just takes great individual practice. The coach must praise great effort and stress defense, and impress on his players that great defensive efforts pay off in victories.

The primary requisites of any successful athletic team are that the team be well conditioned, operate efficiently, and be well disciplined. The great defensive basketball teams, such as Newell's California team, Jucker's Cincinnati teams, Auerbach's Boston Celtics, are teams which were conditioned, had great discipline, and operated efficiently.

It is my contention that a great team defense is built primarily on great individual defense. The basis of any strong team defense is the strength of its man to man defense. At the University of Michigan we use various defenses: straight man to man, zone defenses, half and full court zone press defense, and half and full court man to man defenses. We start, however, by building our defense from a man to man standpoint. I feel very strongly that if we do not master the individual and team man to man defensive principles, we will never master any principles.

A coach makes a critical error if he substitutes a zone defense for his weak man to man and expects it to be any good. Again, I emphasize there are no easy ways to solve this sticky problem of defense. In teaching defense to our team, we emphasize the following 13 defensive principles:

1. We play with weight on the back foot and knees flexed, trunk straight and inclined forward, inside hand up and center of gravity low.
2. Lead with inside foot (one nearest center of floor).
   (a) We do this to challenge outlet passing areas and to *pressure* man with ball.
   (b) This stance enables the player to protect away from help and to protect the base line.
3. Pressure outlet passing areas—we believe in harassment.
4. Retreat to line of ball. The distance a man may leave his man and help out is determined by his own quickness in returning to his man when his man has ball. He must not give this man an unhindered shot.
5. Talk. Communicate with teammates. Vocal support is necessary. It's important that this be stressed to each member of squad. *Make* your team talk when they are playing defense.
   (a) Call switches.
   (b) Tell where offensive post man is playing.
   (c) Call screens from blind side.
   (d) Call if your man is leaving an open spot on floor.

6. We switch on lateral moves, and any other time we must.
   (a) We switch hard to man with ball.
   (b) Our defensive men are taught to come together before they switch.
   (c) We yell when we switch.
7. We try to keep man and ball in sight at all times, but if you lose one you lose the ball—never your man.
8. The defensive man must move every time the ball moves.
9. We allow a two time toward the base line or, if in front, we may two time if opponent with ball has his back to you.
10. Any time a shot is taken, our defensive man's first move is to block his man off the board.
11. Keep hand in shooter's face. Never give an opponent a trouble-free shot if you can help it.
12. When attacking a dribbler, if you go for the ball, do it with your inside hand.
13. Lateral move by defensive man is a type of shuffle. Do not cross feet or bring feet together. We do run after man if he beats us. We try to intercept him at goal, and we teach our boys to head for their defensive basket if they are beaten on a press, as that is where the offensive man is headed.

ZONE

I believe in using a zone strictly as a surprise element and not as a basic defense. It is my conviction that a zone cannot be substituted for a weak man for man and be effective. I also believe that this is the lazy way to coach defense. My premise is that if we have a strong man for man, our zone will be effective. We use it as a last resort. Our zone is a three out, two in, sliding zone, which is sometimes referred to as 1-2-2.

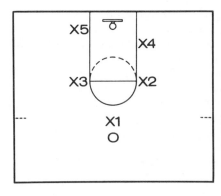

1. Starting position for the three out two back zone with the ball directly out front. X1, X2, and X3 do not play out too far—this is a close, compact zone. With the ball in this position, the two back men, X4 and X5, are not parallel to each other, but one up and the other back. Their position is not predetermined, but these back men talk at all times and change this up and back position when necessary.

2. Ball goes from the center out front to the side. As the ball is passed, each defensive man turns toward the ball and slides to his appropriate defensive position. This is the rule on all passes and shots so that the defensive man will never have his back to the ball. X3 moves out to take man with the ball, X1 slides back to cover the high post, X5 moves halfway out from the basket and the foul line extended. X4 moves into the foul line, and X2 is on the foul line.

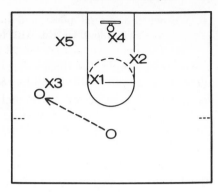

3. Ball moves down the side. X5 takes the ball, X4 moves across keyhole area. X1 drops to cover the pivot from the front. X2 drops to take any cross-court pass. X2 also is responsible to cover the weak side of the board. X3 has option to clamp ball with X5 or drop toward basket to plug the low post area. This second option is recommended for X3, but we do gamble occasionally.

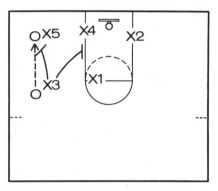

4. On a pass from the front to the high post, X4 moves out to jam from behind. X5 moves behind X4. X3 and X2 form a cup and X1 blitzes from the top. This is a vulnerable spot. Harassment and quickness are needed by the defense.

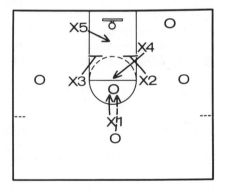

Although we feel this zone gives us the coverage we want, we also recognize its weaknesses. Every man must know his responsibilities and work hard. We stress hands up quick movements of defensive man toward the man with the ball (we fly at him), vocal harassment, and, most of all, hustle. This zone does give us board coverage.

5/8 COURT MAN-TO-MAN PRESS

We operate under the theory that the offensive team appreciates being allowed to operate without undue harassment. Therefore, our cardinal defensive rule is to pester the daylights out of the offense; torment them so that their offense will not operate efficiently and effectively. We have a defensive axiom: treat the offense in the way that you, as an offensive man, *do not* like to be treated.

We teach first and foremost the man-to-man principles which we've stated. Our basic defense is a man-to-man, and our 5/8 court man-to-man is the one we use most.

In addition to the individual and team defensive fundamental rules, we stress the following rules in this defense when we are waiting for them to attack after we score:

1. Our front line defense, guards, attack their guards, who normally have the ball, prior to mid-court and not as far down as the opposition's foul line, hence the 5/8 connotation.
2. If the offensive guard heads to side line with the ball, his defensive man must cut him off and the other defensive guard blitzes from behind.
3. The strong side forward, defensively, plays his man very tight and discourages a pass to him.
4. The defensive high post man cuts off his man as a passing outlet.
5. The weak side forward turns his man loose if he feels he can intercept a pass from guard to guard.
6. If the guard makes a successful pass to the other guard, the defensive corner man on the strong side drops off to help, as does the defensive post man.
7. If the offensive guard dribbles up the middle we blitz with both guards and stop him.
8. Pressure is the keynote, and we scramble back to our man to man when the offense penetrates the press.

The following diagrams help explain the defensive moves in our press.

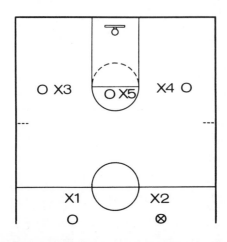

Diagram 1. Our defensive guards X1 and X2 meet the advancing offensive guard in our offensive end of the court, i.e., past mid-court. Our defensive front line, X3, X4, and X5, are parallel with their men and each is alert and aware of the guard action.

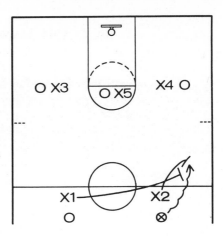

Diagram 2. If the dribbler goes outside, our guard, X2 in this case, moves to cut him off at side line and the blitz is on. X1 releases his man and rushes to two time and trap the ball or X2's man. We try to stop the dribbler just over the ten second line so he's bound on all four sides, two by us, one by the side line, and the other by the ten second line.

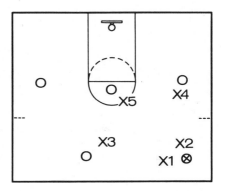

Diagram 3. X3 releases his man, the weak side offensive man, and comes up to pick off any stray pass. X4 covers his man high and tight to choke off the outlet pass. X5 covers post man high to choke off pass to him. If offense penetrates with a pass to any one of the front line we retreat to the basket, and X5 must guard deep basket area.

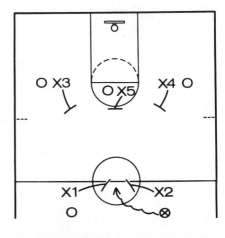

Diagram 4. If the offensive guard tries to penetrate down the middle he is immediately blitzed and stopped by X1 and X2, who harass opponents. X3 and X4 move out between their men and the ball. X5 still cuts off high post.

Remember, once the press is penetrated all the defensive men retreat to stop any easy basket. This press is designed to harass and intimidate the opposition, and take the initiative away from them.

Defensive guards meeting offense at time line.

Strong side defense—outlets pressured.

Offensive guard dribbles to middle and is two-timed by defense.

Ball in corner—five-man defensive alignment.

HALF COURT ZONE PRESS (3-1-1)

In the 1964-65 season we were beaten by a good St. John's team in the finals of the Holiday Festival in New York City. St. John's utilized a half court zone press, 3-1-1 alignment very effectively, and overcame a substantial ten point lead by Michigan to win the game by one point.

In studying the film of this game the next week, we decided this press had excellent merit and that we had personnel on our basketball team adaptable to this defense. We had used a 3-2 half court zone press on previous occasions.

As stated earlier, many of the plans and formations we use are borrowed in this manner. This defense proved very productive for us, and I am sure was responsible in some measure for our success that season.

We put in this defense just prior to our Big Ten season, but did not use it in our opening game. We did use it at some stage in each of our remaining 13 games, however. We would go into this defense after we scored; the signal was a clinched fist held high above our head.

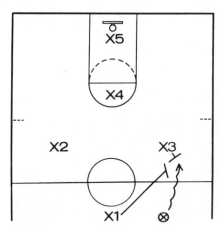

Diagram 1. X1 stations himself in an area at mid-court approximately five to ten feet inside our offensive zone. We invite the offensive guard with the ball to dribble over the ten second line, at which time he is two timed by X1 and X3.

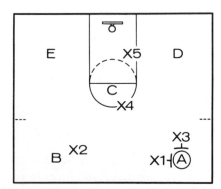

Diagram 2. When A has the ball in this position our rules are as follows: X1 and X3 two time the ball. X4 must cut off any pass to high post area. X5 cheats a little to the strong side and is alert to cut off a pass from A to D. X2 is in position to cut off a pass from A to B.

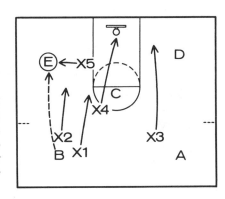

Diagram 3. If A is successful in passing the ball across the court to B, the same rules are in effect. X2 stops the ball and X1 two times. X4 cuts off the high pass. X5 moves to the strong side and X3 is alert to cut off a return pass to A.

Diagram 4. If the offense penetrates our front line of defense with a pass to E, X5 takes him man to man, X4 drops to the basket area, and X1, X2, and X3 move back quickly. We are, in effect, in our 1-2-2 zone, in which we remain until we regain possession of the ball.

The success of this zone depends on all five defense men operating as a unit; it depends a great deal on X1's ingenuity in inviting the offense to dribble across mid-court, and then trapping him; and it depends a great deal on dropping quickly to a zone once the pass has penetrated our front line of defense.

Initial alignment.

Alignment if ball comes down side, i.e., offense moves ball from guard to guard.

Wing man and point man move and trap man with ball.

Trap by middle man and wing man when ball penetrates over time line.

RULES FOR ATTACKING
A HALF COURT ZONE PRESS

The well drilled basketball team must be prepared to face many varied defenses. Among the effective defenses some teams use, including my own, is a half court zone press. Having just explained the way our half court zone defense operates, the following diagrams detail the way our team attacks this press.

Diagram 1. Against this press we send our corner men X3 and X4 in deep and put our center at the high post. We want our team to attack quickly and get to their positions (as shown) quickly.

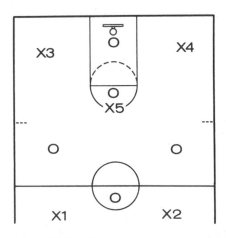

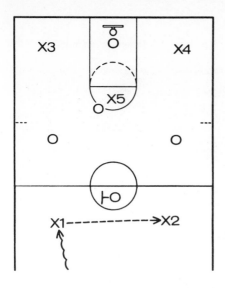

Diagram 2. The guards, one dribbling, attack quickly, but they must stop eight to twelve feet from the ten second line and pass the ball, guard to guard, X1 to X2, to make the defense adjust.

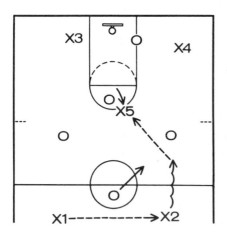

Diagram 3. When X2 receives the ball he drives across the ten second line, trying to penetrate zone's first line of defense, and must release the ball before the zone trap is sprung. X2's first option is to hit X5 if possible, and X5 then turns and tries for the basket, operating as he would on any three on two situation.

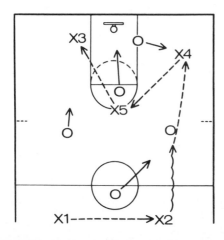

Diagram 4. X2's second option is to hit X4, who then hits X5, and a three on two attack is launched again. X5 tries to hit X3.

Diagram 5. As X2 dribbles quickly ahead he may, as an option, cross-court the ball to X3. This is a difficult pass and may be used only if the defense ignores the weak side corner man completely.

My theory is to attack this zone press, destroy it, and score.

If the zone press is a desperate one, i.e., if they are in a panic defense, we just keep our men spread and move the ball. We will score, of course, but only with layups. Poise and confidence in handling the ball must be evident here. Remember, you have the ball and it is the defense that is in jeopardy.

FULL COURT ZONE PRESS

I don't know who had the original idea for the zone press, but the first time I saw it used, and used effectively, was by Penn State in 1954. Dr. John Lowther of Penn State is credited with its development.

The great UCLA teams of recent vintage have repopularized this press, and its effectiveness is due in great measure to UCLA's great coach, John Wooden, and the dedicated players who performed there. Coach Wooden has stated that he used the zone press some 25 years ago, which would date its origin much earlier than 1954.

In my coaching career we have used two distinct types of full court zone presses, and have also played complete seasons without utilizing either one. My own theory on the use of the zone press and its effectiveness has undergone changes in recent years. In my early years as an assistant and as a head coach I thought it was a great weapon, one that could be of great help as an alternate defense to be used sporadically and effectively. In these early years, in my first exposure to the press, we used a 2-2-1 zone press. After a couple of years we felt that this press was too vulnerable and discontinued the use of any full court zone press, for I had arrived at the erroneous conclusion that the zone press was outmoded, the offense had passed it by, and it was more of a liability than an asset. We continued to utilize our 2-2-1 in practice, but only so that offensively we would be prepared for any team which tried to zone press our club. At this particular stage in my coaching career, I was convinced that the zone press was passé, and that a well drilled, poised, offensive team could destroy any club which dared use it as a basic defense. Needless to say, events which occurred in December of 1963, when we played UCLA in the Los Angeles Classic, and in March of 1965, when we played UCLA in Portland, Oregon, for the National Championship, proved me wrong, as we lost both basketball games by decisive margins. UCLA was very well drilled offensively, as well as defensively, but the zone press was effective. Even prior to playing UCLA I personally had the greatest respect and admiration for Coach John Wooden, and my respect increased after our two meetings.

Our games with UCLA against their press taught us some things relative to the press. Pressuring the man out of bounds seemed sound to us, and when we installed our version of this zone press in the fall of 1965 we incorporated this. Our coaching staff was sold on the merits of this press and, because of this, we were able to sell it to our team. In addition, our talent seemed adaptable to the press. We weren't quite as agile in all five spots as the Uclans, but we weren't bad! The techniques of the press are not difficult to learn, but the dedicated coaching of Wooden, the devilishly determined great play of Goodrich, and the agility of Erickson are not easy to acquire. Successful presses take determined coaching and active players who are disciplined, conditioned, and believe in what they are doing.

MICHIGAN'S 3-1-1 OR 1-2-1-1 FULL COURT ZONE PRESS

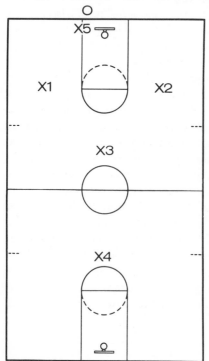

Diagram 1. Basic man alignment: X5, our center, takes the ball and man who is out of bounds. X1 and X2 position themselves at foul line extended and half way from the basket to side line. They put pressure on any offensive man in their area. Either may retreat if no offensive man is in their area. X3 is in our offensive zone, approximately five feet in front of the center circle. X4 is at the opponent's free throw circle.

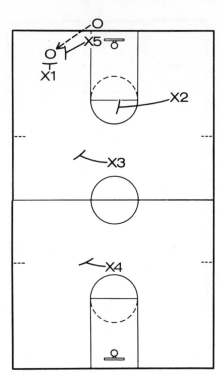

Diagram 2. When ball is passed in bounds, X5 follows pass and two times receiver, with X1 in this case. X2 retreats slightly and moves toward ball, but does not pass center of court. He stays deep if an offensive man is in front of him. X3 moves to side the ball is on and is alert to help out. X4 moves toward strong side but protects deep. If the ball moves parallel to end line, the positions reverse and X5 chases the ball.

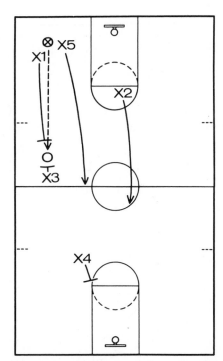

Diagram 3. If pass from in-bounds man goes down side, X3 cuts off man and X1 races to blitz. X2 and X5 race back to defensive positions. X4 retreats to basket area, as he is the safety valve.

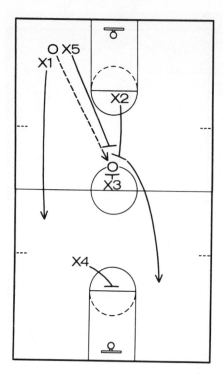

Diagram 4. If pass penetrates to middle man, X3 again cuts off man and X2 blitzes. X4 retreats and is the safety valve. X4 is instructed *never* to go for the ball unless he is 100 per cent sure of intercepting it.

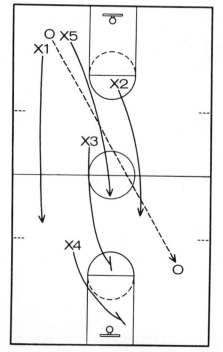

Diagram 5. If pass is thrown cross-court long and complete (this is a very difficult pass and hopefully either X2, X3, or X4 will pick it off), X4 goes to basket, X3 races to high post, and X1, X2, and X5 all retreat for defensive goal.

Initial alignment—fifth man is stationed at top of opponent's foul circle.

Alignment after inbounds pass is received and man with ball is trapped.

Trap and retreat after a pass penetrates front line of defense.

RULES FOR ATTACKING
A FULL COURT ZONE PRESS

The full court pressing defense, both man to man and zone, is much in vogue in basketball now and will become even more important in the future. I feel the game will be played more intensely over the entire court, and the full court defense is responsible for this. Every coach must have a plan for attacking each kind of press.

Early Method of Attacking

For the first four years of my head coaching career we used the following rules in attacking any zone press. The following diagrams explain this method of attack.

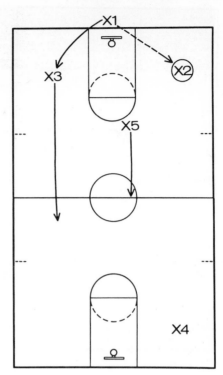

Diagram 1. X1 hits X2 and goes opposite the ball, and replaces X3. X3 and X5
head up the court, running at full speed.
X4 is down the court, having taken this
position immediately after opponent scored
(he takes this position any time your team
feels it may be pressed). **X2** is our best
ball handler.

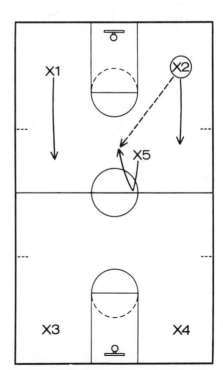

Diagram 2. X2 has the ball; X5 moves
to mid-court and hooks back to a position
midway between the center circle and the
top of the keyhole. X2 hits X5 with the ball
and X1 and X2 move up the court as
quickly as possible and look for a return
pass from X5.

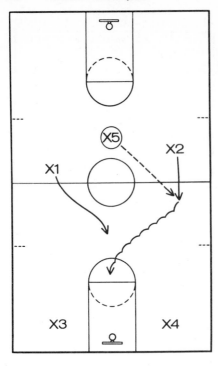

Diagram 3. X5 returns the pass to X2, who dribbles to top of circle. X2, X4, and X3 should have at least a man advantage, and these three men should be able to trigger a high percentage shot. X5 remains back as safety valve, and X1 can trail. We like to have X5 pass the ball rather than turn and dribble, since many teams are instructed to blitz this man whenever he has the ball.

Much has been written about our game with UCLA in the NCAA Finals in March, 1965, in Portland, Oregon. Our team was the number one team in the country according to the final AP and UPI polls. We had lost only three games all year, two by one point each to Nebraska and St. John's, and one to Ohio State when Cazzie Russell was ill and could not play. Our team had advanced to this climactic game by defeating Dayton and a great Vanderbilt team in the Mid-East Regionals, and defeating Princeton in the semi-finals.

UCLA defeated us 91-80 in this final game. They whipped us fair and square, and their zone press was very effective. It might be helpful if I express my views on this game, our plans for attacking the press, our pre-game evaluation of our relative strengths and weaknesses, and what I think actually happened that proved to be Michigan's undoing. Make no mistake about one thing, however. We had a great basketball team, composed of talented, dedicated players, and so did UCLA.

In assessing strengths and weaknesses, we felt that our club should have an edge in strength and rebounding; UCLA should have an edge in over-all team speed. We felt that offensively we were more powerful, and that our defenses were a standoff (this was not true, because theirs was superior that night). We felt the benches were equal, although we feared Ken Washington, and he did come in and hurt us.

Since the semi-finals and finals games are played back to back we could not, nor could they, do much actual playing preparation for the game, but we did walk through our offense against the full court press.

I feel that I made one critical error in coaching that night by not following my own game plan, which was to give my two biggest players, Bill Buntin (6' 7", 230) and Oliver Darden (6' 7", 225) a periodic rest, regardless of the score. I intended to substitute for them after seven or eight minutes of elapsed time in each half. This I did not do, and I think it hurt us.

It is my opinion, and I'd guess that this opinion is shared by many, that Wooden outcoached me that night. I believe that he was able to read our method of attacking his press. We did have early success, but after a UCLA time-out, with about ten minutes gone and Michigan leading, they seemed to choke off our outlets and neutralize our zone press offense. This was one important item which led to our downfall. They also outshot us, were equal on the boards, played a spirited game, and deserved to win. Gail Goodrich was magnificent that night, and if any one individual was instrumental in our demise it was he.

Good things come from defeat. We felt we needed new offensive plans to combat the full court zone press, and that the UCLA zone press was a good one, so we copied it to the best of our ability and used it with success the following season.

Current Method of Attacking

In 1965-66 we installed the following method of attacking a zone press. We feel this is better than the one previously described in that it:

1. Attacked quicker.
2. Was not as stereotyped, in that any one of three men could handle the ball in bounds.
3. Gave us more options of advancing the ball and more safety valves.
4. Had more movement by all the players, and wasn't dependent on one any more than any other.

The following diagrams explain this offense.

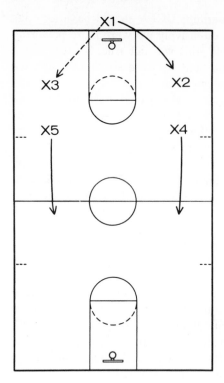

Diagram 1. Either X1, X2, or X3, our quickest forward, is instructed to take the ball out of bounds and get it in quickly. X1 hits X3 and goes opposite. X4 and X5 race to mid-court, stop, and look to hook back as outlet man.

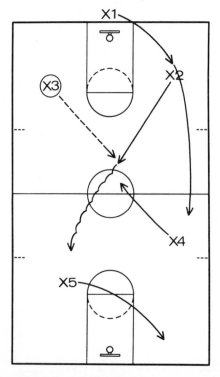

Diagram 2. X3 has ball, X1 replaces X2, X2 sprints diagonally across toward X5 and looks for return pass. X4 cuts hard for center of the court as outlet man (he's the big man opposite the initial receiver, X3). X5 moves to opposite side. X3 hits X2 as first option, and X2 heads up court with ball, as do all players without ball.

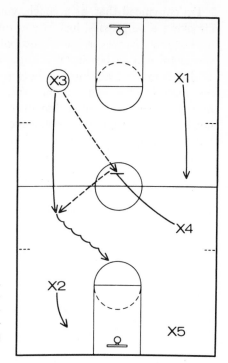

Diagram 3. If X3 hits X2, then the attack is on. If X3 can't hit X2 he looks for X4, hits him, and X3 and X1 head up court and look for return. If X2 and X4 are not open, X1 must be, and X3 can hit him and advance from there.

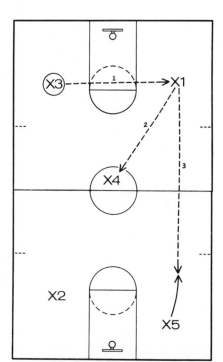

Diagram 4. If X2 and X4 are not open, then X1, who has replaced X2, must be, and X3 returns the ball to him. X1 may advance by dribbling, or he may hit X4 or X5.

I'm convinced that, as a coach, you must give your team a method of attacking zone presses, just as you must coach your team in every phase of the game. However, speed and poise can beat the zone press, and any successful way of beating it is a good one. As I stated, I believe that the UCLA team of 1965 hurt us because we were a bit too stereotyped in our method of advancing the ball; a team must be able to use some initiative. The basic plan, however, must exist and be developed. I do not believe in complete freelancing against the zone press, or any press, but I do feel the method of attacking it must be rather fluid.

CHAPTER 6

Aspects of the Game

PRESSURE BASKETBALL

When defense is spoken of in this day and age, pressure seems to be one of the key words. The evolution of the game of basketball, and particularly of the shooter and the escalation of shooting percentages, has made basketball coaches view their defenses with a much more practiced eye. It is difficult to say which coach or coaches first used the tough full court pressure defense, but men such as Phog Allen of Kansas, Hank Iba of Oklahoma State, and Pete Newell of California come to my mind as men who have used various types of pressure defenses to make their basketball teams successful.

Even though the offensive prowess of teams, and the offensive abilities of individual players, are spotlighted in the press and other publicity vehicles, it is my opinion that defensive basketball is being emphasized more than ever by competent basketball coaches, and that we will continue to see improvement in defensive play.

The defensive trend seems to be to utilize all of the players, all of the time, in the defense. This means that basketball coaches are moving their men further and further down court in order to make the team which has the ball work hard all of the time. I feel this is an excellent trend as it makes for a more active, action-packed game, but it does mean that the teams must be better drilled, conditioned, and disciplined than ever before. This is true whether the reference is to offense or defense.

Another trend seems to be to put pressure on the offense so that they never have a moment to relax with the ball. Previously teams were able to advance the ball, leisurely, at their own pace, as long as they crossed the center line within ten seconds, but the great defensive teams do not allow this any more. As I have mentioned previously, however the attack is organized, whether full or half court zone pressure, full or half court man to man pressure, it is imperative that the successful basketball team be prepared to meet the various types of pressure defenses, often involving several different kinds in any one game. Our rules are as follows:

1. We want our club to attack with speed, thereby avoiding any type of pressure.
2. We want to attack any full court press with the idea of destroying it, and never want to be satisfied just to advance the ball over the ten second line.
3. We want to keep the floor balanced.
4. If the pressure defense is straight man to man, we are inclined to give the ball to one of our guards and allow him to advance it by a dribble on a one and one situation. Don't forget, the most adequate defensive player cannot stop the offensive player if the offensive player has any room in which to maneuver.
5. If we find two defensive men on the ball, we let one advance by a pass and then have the passer advance himself by a sprint.
6. We want players to always face their offensive basket. It is a cardinal sin if we let any defensive man turn any of our players around.
7. Remain poised. The only way I know to assure your basketball club of being poised in any situation is by constant drilling on these situations, so that in the course of a game nothing can take you by surprise.
8. Be active without the ball.
9. Don't let the defense dictate to you what you are going to do or at what pace the game will be played.
10. Be physically and mentally ready to play a tough 40 minutes of basketball, and be ready to play this all on the court if necessary.
11. Be prepared.

I have previously explained how we exert the actual pressure, and

I am certain that you can diagram a pattern which will operate similarly against each and every pressure. Some coaches feel that they have a bona fide plan for attacking every type of press, but we have actually never come across any system which, by itself, would be successful. The team which can play a good tough pressure defense is a team which is disciplined, conditioned, and aggressive. The team which can attack the pressure successfully is the one which combines these ingredients with poise. Our goal is, of course, to combine all of the ingredients into one basketball team so that we are strong both offensively and defensively.

BASKETBALL PLAYERS

Basketball, by its very nature, is a long, tedious, demanding game which requires a great deal of mental and physical discipline from the boys playing the game. There is, necessarily, a very close relationship between the players and the coaches, as a varsity squad normally consists of approximately 15 ball players who are with their coach or coaches for about six months out of the year.

The basic requisite of a basketball player is that he have a genuine love of the game. Only by thoroughly enjoying the playing and practicing of basketball can a player make the physical and mental sacrifices required for any type of success to be achieved. A player has to respect his coach and honestly believe that the coach is working on his and on his teammates' behalf. Love of the game cannot be manufactured artificially, and if a player does not genuinely enjoy basketball then his chances of succeeding are nil.

As a coach, I give our players certain terms which they must accept if they are to play basketball for the University of Michigan. They have an opportunity to discuss these terms if they feel they are unfair. We impress on our young men that it is a privilege and an honor to represent our school on the basketball floor, and that they should willingly make sacrifices in order to gain the many benefits which will accrue to them from playing. From a training standpoint, we state that they are to abstain completely from tobacco and alcohol. They must agree to expend a great deal of energy in order to achieve the necessary physical condition to play this very exhausting game. We demand, as well as the University, of course, that they be in good academic standing. One of our conditions is that they attend every class and develop study habits which will enable them to pass the course, not only satisfactorily but with an effort to excel academically. We also impress on our young men that they represent a great university, and consequently we want them to maintain a neat and immaculate appearance, both on and off the basketball floor. We do not tolerate any slovenly attire. We do not try to dictate fashion to our ball club, but we do demand that they be well groomed.

We demand punctuality from our players. We want them on the basketball floor at a particular time, and they must be there. We have a definite itinerary which must be followed to the minute when we are making trips. Tardiness is a luxury a basketball team can ill afford.

We expect our players to give us 100 per cent effort at all times, on the practice floor, in the classroom, on trips, and during games. I repeat that basketball is a simple game. The basketball slogan by which we live at Michigan is very simple: Hard work equals victory.

Players will differ in their talents; some will be bigger and stronger, some will be better rebounders and better shooters, but everyone can be equal in the amount of effort expended for a common goal. The basketball coach must expect and demand this great effort from his team; if he is successful in getting it, winning will become a habit.

We want our players to know that each one is extremely important to the over-all success of the ball club. We don't like to divide our team into regulars and substitutes. I don't designate our players as first, second, or third teams, and never call them out on the floor in that manner. I think the coach must strive very hard to treat everyone alike. I realize that some players are more important to the success of the team than others, but for the good of the ball club each player must realize that he is an important cog in the wheel.

The coach is paid to be a critic of the team. We want our basketball players to be all for one and one for all. We don't allow any of our players to grimace or criticize another player on the ball club. We want our players to take a positive approach, smiling or giving a note of recognition when one boy on our team makes an exceptionally good pass or shot.

This one for all and all for one theory must be understood by the players on the ball club if success is going to be obtained. As coaches we try to avoid any type of clique within our club. When we travel on the road we rotate roommates on every trip. We will also change the weekly shooting partners in the early part of practice, so that everybody becomes dependent on everybody else. As long as they keep score in basketball, the players should relish victory when victory accrues to their team. No one should enjoy or expect defeat, but, more important, no one should ever complain or blame another player on his team when defeat occurs. At the risk of being repetitious, I again inject a note about the intangible influence of enthusiasm. The enthusiastic player is a happy player, and an enthusiastic player is normally an efficient player. We want our ball club to be both happy and efficient.

We build a strong player-coach relationship by emphasizing the following points with our players:

1. The successful player must love the game, and basketball must be very important to him. If it is not important to the young player, he will not make the sacrifices which must be made in order to succeed.
2. Each player is important to the over-all picture. We emphasize that all players can't do things equally well, all can't be a Cazzie Russell or Jerry West, but each player can do something to contribute, and must do what he can at 100 per cent of his ability.
3. Be "up" for practice. The will to win is not as important as the will to prepare to win. It is easy to be "up" for a game with the crowd, band, and contagious excitement, but the great players practice as hard as they play.
4. Think positively. If you think you can, you can.
5. Play with *enthusiasm*. Enthusiasm is the most important of the intangible assets, and genuine enthusiasm will generate victory.
6. We ask each player to ask himself one question—How good do I want to be? Any player setting his goals high can achieve success. The human body can accomplish many things if the mind will dictate to the body how much it wants to accomplish.

Cazzie Russell, Michigan's three time All-American and the nation's outstanding collegiate player in 1966, is an example of basketball greatness. The game is of the utmost importance to him and he dearly loves playing. Cazzie made all of the physical sacrifices in order to be in the best possible physical condition, and he worked hard and trained hard because basketball playing was fun.

Russell thrilled many people in this country with his excellent play. He thrilled me in each game he played, but, what is more important, he thrilled me in practice. He was always industrious. As a two time All-American in his senior year at our school he still worked as hard as anyone, never was careless (he respected the game too much), and always played with genuine enthusiasm.

Russell was the greatest collegiate player in the land because this was his goal. He had great God-given natural talents, but no player ever worked harder than Cazzie to develop these talents. Cazzie was a positive thinker and never understood when we lost, although he never made excuses. He expected victories, worked hard to provide them, and he produced many in his three years on our varsity.

It is true that the Cazzie Russells are few and far between, and I'll forever be grateful that Cazzie Russell came along in my lifetime, but I maintain that any player with the proper attitude can accomplish a great deal.

Russell spotlighted the phrase, "There is not much between mediocrity and talent; merely a decimal point called application."

BASKETBALL PRACTICE

The real, earnest, down-to-earth coaching occurs during the practice session. The time a basketball team practices is the most important time of the season, as far as the players and coaches are concerned. It is during this time the players are developed, trained, and become disciplined, and the team as a whole is developed and nurtured. Every player on every team hopes to win; however, the team, players, and coaches who have the determined will to *prepare* to win are the ones to whom victory will accrue.

Real coaching is done during the practice session, for it is during this period that basketball games are actually won and lost. The most important law under which we operate at the University of Michigan is that a player plays in games as he practices. We do not believe in the so-called "Saturday basketball player." In my judgment, this is nonsense, and I have never seen a basketball player perform creditably in games who has not performed well in practice. I think it's true that some players on occasion rise to greatness, respond very well to the challenges that competition gives them, and play very fine basketball in competitive games. It's been my good fortune to coach a number of young men who fall in this category. Cazzie Russell, whom I have mentioned frequently in this book, performed almost miraculously during the 1964-65 season in a number of very close basketball games and was responsible for our team winning these games in the last three or four minutes. Cazzie Russell, however, is my prime example of a young man who made himself a great All-American basketball player by his diligent work on the practice floor.

As I have mentioned earlier, organization and practice are of the utmost importance. These sessions must be organized in detail, minute by minute, in order that your coaching job is accomplished. You must be organized to insure that your team is prepared to play to the best of its ability at all times.

Timewise, our practices are organized so that, prior to our first game, we have two hours of organized work per day, with a minimum of 15 minutes of free shooting. Actually, there is no such thing as free shooting, since the coach is always there to supervise any player on the basketball floor. It is a cardinal rule with me that a coach must be the first one on the practice floor. In this way, it becomes the coach's responsibility to see that bad habits are avoided. In our situation, we have six weeks in which to prepare, October 15 to December 1, and we operate on this two hour basis during these weeks. After our opening game, we cut our practice sessions to one hour and a half, plus the 15 minutes of shooting. I might mention that this 15 minutes is the minimum and we expect our team, if their academic classes allow, to get in a minimum of one-half hour of shooting per day. On the day prior to games, we work just one hour.

Punctuality is the byword at the University of Michigan, and each player conforms to our rules concerning this most important item. We have no patience with the young man who is late to our practice sessions. If a player has a legitimate reason for being late, we take this into consideration, of course. No player is allowed on our basketball floor after 4:00 P.M. unless he sees me personally and gives me the reason why he was detained. It is up to the coach to either accept or reject these reasons. I've made it a rule of thumb to accept the reasons for one tardiness; however, if the boy comes late the second time then it's my rule to dismiss him from practice on that day. By missing practice he misses a chance to improve himself, and consequently the person most hurt is the player.

Regardless of the time you start practice, each player must be ready to practice by that time. By ready to practice, we mean that our players must be fully dressed in practice uniform, taped, shoes laced, and on the floor shooting. As stated, our practices begin at 4:00 P.M. and our organized practice begins at 4:15 P.M.

Seriousness of purpose is the keynote of our practice sessions. Adolph Rupp, the renowned coach at Kentucky, has made the statement that he does not allow a team to talk while they are on the practice floor. I see much merit in Coach Rupp's rule, and although we do not go quite that far, we do demand that there be no nonsense during the time our team is engaged in basketball practice. We expect each player to improve every day, and the only way you can improve is through diligent work. Basketball is a game of habits, and it is during these practice sessions that players develop correct ones.

Activity is extremely important, and we do not want our players inactive at any time during the practice sessions. If some of the players are not participating in particular drills, or in our team offense or team defense, we still demand that they be very attentive. We continually stress attention to detail, because the basketball team which pays attention to each detail will be a winning ball club.

You will note in the six week practice plan which follows that we do not scrimmage a great deal. We never scrimmage just for the sake of scrimmaging, but to accomplish certain things: conditioning, the moulding of our offense and defense, and the feeling of playing together. If a coach finds himself scrimmaging just to fill up his practice time, he is going to be a loser and is not doing the job for which he is paid.

After the first month of practice, our scrimmage consists of game situations which we run with the clock and scoreboard in operation. We try to simulate every situation which could arise in the course of the game. Most of these are game closing situations, such as our team being two points ahead with two minutes to play and possession of the basketball, or the converse of that situation. We feel that a knowledge of what to do in every situation will produce victory. Luck has very little to do with winning or losing. It has been my experience in the years I have coached that the good teams are the lucky teams.

Basketball season is long and tedious. The basketball practice and games are very demanding, physically and mentally, on the players. We want our practices to be interesting and to have a recognizable goal that our players can understand. We feel that humor on occasion can be wonderful therapy, and although we do not allow horseplay during our practices we do encourage fun at practice. We want our players to enjoy practice, have fun without being funny, and benefit each day from the one to two hours of organized work that they spend in improving their game.

It's the coach's job to prepare his team to the best of his ability. I have found that boys like to work, want to learn, and are willing to work hard if they are able to see their objective. I have also found that players on college and high school teams are intelligent young men and, individually and collectively, are able to recognize if their practice sessions are accomplishing anything. No one person can successfully prepare his team to meet every emergency which arises during the course of each basketball game, but any man worthy of the title "coach" can do his utmost to see that his team is well prepared. The successful basketball coach must be dedicated to his sport, well organized, a tireless worker, and in the process of continually improving and adding to his own knowledge of the game.

On the following pages are shown the daily work plans of our basketball team from October 18 to November 30, 1965. These plans are somewhat condensed, but they do emphasize a most important point, that every detail of each practice session must be organized and planned to the minute.

DAILY ORGANIZATION PLANS
PRE-SEASON OCTOBER 18—NOVEMBER 30, 1965

October 18

4:00- 4:15	Get ready—shoot quickly
4:15- 4:35	2 lines—ball
	3 lines—figure 8, no shoot
	5 lines—figure 8, no shoot
4:35- 4:45	3 line short shot drill
4:45- 4:55	Pepper drill
4:55- 5:10	Fouls and Moby's drill
5:10- 6.00	3 on 2—1 way
	3 on 2—both ways
	3 on 3—break
6:00- 6:10	Slides and hands up

October 19

4:00- 4:15	Get ready
4:15- 4:30	Offensive drills
	1) forward pivot and follow drill
	2) forward back cut drill
4:30- 5:15	Offense
	1) Tight all options
	2) Popeye—double cut
	3) Offense and defense vs. break
5:15- 5:30	Defensive slides and 1 on 1—no hands
5:30- 5:45	2 on 1—half court
	2 on 1—full court
5:45- 6:00	3 on 2—full court
	3 on 3—full court
6:00- 6:06	Hands up

October 20

4:00- 4:15	Warm up
4:15- 4:30	Slides
	1 on 1
	Jumping drill
4:30- 5:10	Forward and guard defense
	1 on 1—outlet
	2 on 2—outlet
	Guard-guard
	Corner-post
	Rebounding
	Pressure and switch tough
5:10- 5:25	Fouls—50

5:25- 5:55	Defense and break
5:55- 6:05	Hands up
	Jim's drill

October 21

4:00- 4:15	Get ready
4:15- 4:35	Clear move
	Popeye move
	Quick move with trailer
4:35- 5:15	Offense—post man starting low
	Tight
	Popeye
	Quick
5:15- 5:40	3 on 3 half court and full court (offense & defense)
5:40- 5:50	Fouls—50
5:50- 6:05	Run and slides
	1 on 1

October 22

4:00- 4:15	Get ready
4:15- 4:30	Slides
	2 line shot drill (short shot)
4:30- 4:40	Ball handling—4 corner and in file
4:40- 5:15	1 on 1
	3 line short shot drill
	Fouls
5:15- 6:00	Scrimmage
6:00- 6:10	Run

October 25

4:00- 4:15	Get ready
4:15- 4:30	Fast break drill
	Shooting drills
4:30- 4:45	Rebounding—offensive and defensive
4:45- 5:00	Corner defense
	Guard pass in to forward
5:00- 5:10	Slides and 1 on 1
5:10- 5:20	Fouls
5:20- 6:00	Defense
6:00- 6:10	Run

October 26

4:00- 4:15	Get ready
	W.S. defense
4:15- 4:30	Ball handling and shooting
4:30- 5:00	2 on 1
	3 on 2
	3 on 3
5:00- 5:45	Offense

	2-3—tight and quick
	Popeye—add clear—inside—hand off
5:45- 6:00	Fouls
6:00- 6:05	Run—slides

October 27

4:00- 4:15	Get ready
4:15- 4:25	Run—slides
4:25- 4:40	3 man break drill
4:40- 4:50	5 man break
	Ball handling
	Run
4:50- 5:15	Defense vs. freshmen (break)
5:15- 5:40	Offense vs. freshmen (no break)
5:40- 6:00	Scrimmage

October 28

4:00- 4:10	Shoot and get ready
4:10- 4:15	Talk
4:15- 4:40	Ball handling
	4 corner drill
	In file
	Ball handling drill
	Change of direction drill
4:40- 5:00	Fouls—make 25
5:00- 5:40	Offense and defense
5:40- 5:50	Run

October 29

4:00- 4:15	Get ready
4:15- 4:30	Jog, sprint, jump
4:30- 4:45	Defense vs. #3
4:45- 4:55	Scrimmage—#1 vs. #2
4:55- 5:50	Scrimmage—varsity vs. freshmen

October 30

| 10:00-11:00 | Shoot-run-foul game |
| | Break drills |

November 1

4:00- 4:15	Get ready
4:15- 4:30	Run and shoot drills
	Full court and half court
4:30- 5:00	2 on 1
	3 on 2
	3 on 3
	Half and full court
5:00- 5:15	Fouls—25
5:15- 6:00	Defense—full court man to man and weak and half court man to man

6:00- 6:10	Run

November 2

4:00- 4:15	Get ready
4:15- 4:30	Slides and run and shoot
4:30- 5:00	Offense vs. varsity
	add strong
	add number
	add Red
5:00- 5:10	Fouls
5:10- 5:40	Offensive vs. freshmen (possession)
5:40- 5:55	Scrimmage—full court man to man press after score
5:55- 6:05	Run

November 3

4:00- 4:15	Get ready
4:15- 4:30	Slides
	Ball handling—long pass—3 man weave
	Short shots—receiving ball drill
4:30- 4:45	3 on 3—half court and full court
4:45- 5:00	4 on 4 both ways
5:00- 5:15	Fouls
5:15- 5:55	Defense vs. freshmen

November 4

4:00- 4:15	Get ready
4:15- 4:30	Run and jump
	Driving and receiving drill
	Run and shoot drill
4:30- 4:45	Moby's drill
	Slides
	Hands up
4:45- 5:00	3 on 3
	Rebound and run
5:00- 5:10	Fouls
5:10- 5:50	Offense—no break
	Attack full court
5:50- 6:05	Run

November 5

4:00- 4:30	Warm up
4:30- 5:50	Scrimmage

November 8

4:00- 4:15	Pressure—corner men
4:15- 4:30	Slides and run and jump
4:30- 4:50	Ball handling—in file—4 corner
	2 lines shooting
4:50- 5:20	2 on 1

	3 on 2
	3 on 3
5:20- 5:30	Fouls
5:30- 5:50	4 on 4—pressure and two time
5:50- 6:00	Run

November 9

4:00- 4:15	Get ready
4:15- 4:45	Run and shoot—full court
	Defense
	1) corner pressure
	2) guards pressure
	3) guard and forward
	Defense—slide through
4:45- 5:15	Offense vs. man to man defense
5:15- 6:00	Put in zone defense and put in man to man pressure to a zone
6:00- 6:10	Run

November 10

No practice—Toledo Clinic

November 11

4:00- 4:15	Defense—corner
4:15- 4:30	Fast break drills—competitive
4:30- 5:00	Defense—pressure to zone and man to man
5:00- 6:00	Scrimmage

November 12

4:00- 4:45	Shoot hard
	3 on 3 front line
	Slides—1 on 1—run
	3 on 3—rebound
4:45- 5:45	Defense and break
	man to man zone
	zone press to zone
	full court man to man
5:45- 6:00	Shoot fouls and run
	4 at each basket, 2 at a time with one Jim's between

November 13

Offense—review

November 15

4:00- 4:15	Get ready
4:15- 4:45	Run—jump—slides
	3 on 2—2 on 1
4:45- 5:00	Fouls—10 without a miss
5:00- 5:20	3 on 3
	rebound and run if miss

full court press if shot made

5:20- 5:50   4 on 4

defend and run

communicate

5:50- 6:00   Run

November 16

4:00- 4:30   Get ready

Run and shoot

Put in stall game

4:30- 5:30   Situation

    1) 10 minute scrimmage

    2) 5 minute segments

    3) 2 minute segments

5:30- 5:40   Fouls

5:40- 5:55   Break drills and run Jim's drill

5:55- 6:00   Make 5 fouls in a row

November 17

4:00- 4:45   1) Run and shoot and slides

    2) Jump ball

    3) End line

    4) 3 on 3 (press full court)

4:45- 5:45   1) 10 minute scrimmage

    2) 5 minute segments

    3) 3 minute segments

    emphasis 2-3

    press full court man for man and use fist up

5:45- 5:55   Fouls

5:55- 6:05   Sprints

November 18

4:00- 4:30   Run and shoot and loosen up

4:30- 5:15   Offense vs. defense and break

#1 and #2 vs. #3

5:15- 5:45   Defense—possession #1 vs. #2

Man to man and fists up

5.45- 6:05   Delay—offense

Desperate pressure—defense

November 19

4:00- 4:30   Get ready

4:30- 5:30   Scrimmage

5:30- 5:50   Delay game

November 24

4:00- 4:15   Get ready (post defense)

4:15- 4:45	Slides
	1 on 1 full court
	2 on 2 full court
	3 on 3 full court
4:45- 5:15	Offense vs. zone
	1) smash offensive board
	2) strong—number—high
5:15- 5:25	Fouls—30 (must make 24)
5:25- 6:00	Defense—full court man to man pressure
	Half court pressure
6:00- 6:05	Run

November 25

10:00-10:15	Warm up
10:15-10:30	Fast break drills
10:30-11:15	Offense vs. zones
11:15-12:00	Defense—full and half court zone press
12:00-12:10	Fouls and run

November 26

3:00- 3:45	Get ready
	Tennessee—defense against
	Quickness drills
3:45- 5:00	Offense and defense—review all presses
5:00- 5:15	Run and fouls

November 27

9:30-10:00	Warm up
	Fast break drills
10:00-11:00	Scrimmage
	Yellow team—zone
	Blue team—full court man to man pressure
	Blue team—zone press to a zone after score
11:00-11:15	Fouls—50 (5 in a row)

November 29

4:30- 5:00	Get ready (running and ball handling drills)
5:00- 5:30	Offense vs. zone
	Offense vs. man to man
	Stall offense
5:30- 6:00	Defense
	man to man full court
	zone press—half and full
	2-2-1 zone
6:00- 6:15	Run—fouls

November 30

| 4:00- 4:30 | Get ready |

Run and shoot

4:30- 5:15   Review

    1) stall

    2) zone offense

    3) Tennessee offense

5:15- 5:40   Fouls

5 man break

Hit one from each side

    We like to dwell on many different scrimmage situations, for in many instances games are won or lost by the margin of a small detail. In the heat of battle, in the close, hard fought game, the players look to their coach for leadership, and the successful, well prepared coach provides it. The well prepared team has found itself in a similar circumstance in practice, and this practice can pay off.

    The following types of typical situation basketball are emphasized and practiced at Michigan, with the Blue team designated as the Michigan squad. Our assistant coach has the Yellow squad and he may do what he wishes.

1. *Score*—Blue 86, Yellow 85

   Time—Three minutes left to play in the game

   Situation—Blue player at foul line with two shots

   Coaching action—Our coaching point here would be to say that if we, "Michigan," got possession of the ball with any lead we should go into a dead stall game and shoot only layups or fouls. If we get a tie with less than a minute to go we should hold for the last shot and run a clear with ten seconds left. If we should lose the lead we must press full court man to man.

2. *Score*—Blue 85, Yellow 86

   Time—Two minutes left to play in the game

   Situation—Yellow player at foul line, one and one situation

   Coaching action—(a) Defense: Blue to utilize full court zone press after a blue score *if* they are behind. If Yellow penetrates press past mid-court Blue drops into a desperate man to man pressure defense.

   (b) Offense: When we get ball we will be either one, two, or three points behind, so we must go to score quickly. If and when we get the lead we will pull out of the full court zone press and pick up the Yellow team at half court with normal man to man.

3. *Score*—Blue 91, Yellow 91

   Time—20 seconds to play

   Situation—Blue player at foul line, one and two situation

   Coaching action—(a) Defense: When Yellow gets ball the score will be tied or Blue ahead. We will pick up Yellow offense at mid-court, tough, and harass to keep them from high percentage shot.

   (b) Offense: If ahead when we get the ball, stall. If behind, and Yellow scores quickly, get time out and go for the shot.

4. *Score*—Blue 84, Yellow 80
   Time—Four minutes to play
   Situation—Blue ball at mid-court
   Coaching action—Drive, delay to score. At two minutes with same or increased lead, stall.
5. *Score*—Blue 90, Yellow 89
   Time—30 seconds to play
   Situation—Blue ball out of bounds at mid-court
   Coaching action—Get ball into play and set up a stall offense. If defense is in half court zone press, spot offense and look for back cutters and layups.

It is evident that many different situations could occur, and we try to simulate all. We work on these during the last 20 to 30 minutes of practice when the element of fatigue is apparent in both clubs. We use the game clock and try to have competent officials.

The results of these scrimmages are evident, I think, and they do make for increased poise and efficiency, and help the players to make a more courageous, prompt, and positive response to the many tough challenges that basketball affords.

SUBSTITUTIONS

An important part of successful basketball coaching, and an integral part of the successful operation of any team, is the thoughtful and efficient use of substitution. This operation begins prior to the actual substitution act during a game. It is a vital part of the team's and the coach's philosophy, and it is necessary that every player on the squad feels that he is important. If this attitude is prevalent, the job of substituting is easy, because all the players are ready, eager, and willing to play. It is important to live by the motto that a basketball team is not divided into regulars and substitutes. It is vital that each player be 100 per cent-plus in the basketball game, whether or not he is physically playing.

The players on the bench during the course of the contest should be on the edge of their seats, studying men they may be called on to guard, and immediately ready to play if the coach beckons them. It is difficult to go into a game as a substitute, and therefore adequate mental preparation is most necessary. A substitute has to be ready to at least maintain the tempo of the game—preferably, he should pick up the tempo. In other words, he must be prepared to go from absolute immobility into high gear without the benefit of even warming up.

The coach will substitute for the following reasons: If a player is injured, he would naturally be replaced. It is important to replace a tired player with a fresh one. A coach must judge whether one of his boys is having an off night and if someone else will do a better job.

Substitution should be made if a situation presents itself during the course of a game whereby someone on your bench can be an advantage—by injecting more speed against a press, providing better outside shooting against a sagging zone defense, correcting a mismatch in size, and so on. A coach must decide if he wants to substitute to change the tempo of the game, which he sometimes must do in order to control it.

When foul trouble overcomes one or more players it is important to consider replacing them. There is no easy way to decide when a substitution should be made for a player who becomes burdened with fouls. We follow these rules of thumb, but actually the particular game itself dictates when substitutions should be made. We like to avoid the fourth foul in the first half. I have come to the conclusion that, unless it can benefit our club to substitute, we will play a player with four fouls anytime from 20 minutes on. It is worth the calculated risk to play a player with four fouls, even with the possibility of losing him, than to place him on the bench where, in effect, he is lost already.

All of the players on the team should be expected to want to play—to want to start. But even if they don't start they must be in the proper frame of mind to be ready to play at any time. We want our substitute to enter the game with enthusiasm, making verbal contact with the man he replaces so that the substitute will know who *his* man is. We want the player leaving the floor to leave it quickly, go directly to the coach, and take a seat next to him.

We can never allow a bench full of relaxed, lazy basketball players. We never want to see any feet crossed on the bench, for if the men are relaxed there they are relaxed out in the game. Remember, when you substitute, you substitute to improve your play, not just to carry on.

HALF-TIME PROCEDURES

We believe the half-time interval is a most important part of the game, and that if the time is properly budgeted much can be accomplished in the ten or twelve minutes available to the basketball coach. We like to break our half-time into three distinct phases.

The first phase is the first three or four minutes of rest for our players, at which time the coaches can consult and review the statistics of the first half, if such are available. This is also a time when the coach can collect his thoughts and plan in his mind what he is going to say to his team.

The second segment is given to constructive criticism of the team's play in the first half. I don't believe an emotional outburst by the coach at any time serves any useful purpose. However, it is important that the coach focus on errors of commission or omission, and analyze and discuss reasons why the play is going either well or badly. It is also important that the individual players be criticized, constructively, if the need for criticism is apparent.

The third, and most important, period is the last four or five minutes, when a constructive plan for the second half must be presented. Of course, if things are going well in the first half the plan is merely continued. If, however, the team seems to be sputtering and malfunctioning, it is up to the coach to issue a new type of offense or defense or do something to get the club on a more productive plane.

It is my feeling that individual members of the team must remain silent during the half-time procedures unless they have some constructive comment or question to ask. It has been my policy on occasion to interrogate a particular player, and in many instances these players come up with excellent ideas as to changes which might be made within the over-all picture of our defense and offense. These changes have often proven to be beneficial.

I like to send our team back on the floor with the knowledge of what they are to do in the second half, and to give them a minimum of three minutes in which to warm up. It has been my policy to be notified by the timer at the five minute mark so I can conclude whatever comments I want to make and still send them out with ample time to warm up.

SCOUTING

Scouting has become an important part of the over-all basketball picture. At Michigan, we believe it is worthwhile, and make every effort to have a member of our staff scout an opponent at least once. We like to try to see the Big Ten teams twice, as the second look is helpful in confirming the conclusions of the first look.

Scouting is worth it if it can either help you make one extra basket, or prevent your opponent from scoring one. This is our basic premise. Remember, forewarned is forearmed.

In a broad sense we want our scout to arrive at two simple conclusions relative to the team he has scouted:

1. Where can they most likely hurt us?
2. Where can we most likely hurt them?

We like to have our scout come up with the following information regarding the opponent's team operation:

1. Scouted game and cumulative statistics.
2. Analysis of over-all team speed.

3. Team's basic offensive operation vs. the type of defense we might employ.
4. Their delay or stall game, if they exposed it.
5. Their jump ball alignments.
6. A calculated guess as to their over-all team poise and their over-all team thinking ability and mental and physical condition.
7. All out of bounds maneuvers.
8. Analysis of their hustle and industry.
9. Basic defensive plan:
    (a) Alignment.
    (b) Where do they meet the offense after they score?
    (c) Ability to break from offense to defense.
    (d) How do they, as a team, defend the end line at the opponent's basket
       —zone, switching man to man, straight man to man?
10. Game shot charts (we do not expect our scout to keep the chart).

We want the following information concerning each individual opponent:

1. Game and cumulative statistics.
2. Speed—forward, lateral, backward, and speed with and without the ball.
3. Favorite shooting areas and favorite shots.
4. Maneuvering ability, with and without the ball.
5. Defensive analysis:
    (a) Movement.
    (b) Eyes—is he a ball watcher?
    (c) Hustler?
6. Physical condition.
7. If a post defender, where does he guard the center—front, behind, side, etc.?
8. Rebounding ability.
9. Courage.
10. Poise.

We want a general opinion of our opponent and an honest appraisal of our chances. Actually, I believe that many scouts return with an overabundance of information, which only clouds the issue. The simple, complete report is the best.

We utilize this information and always give it to our players verbally; many times we even give out mimeographed information. We neither over- nor undersell our opponent, and we never underestimate the ability of the five young men playing for the other club.

We like to send our own scouts, as they have a knowledge of our team, and scout with our team in mind. We have used scouting bureaus when distance, time, or scheduling precluded our taking a personal look. I have found some of these reports to be very good.

We deem it important that the scout write up his report as quickly as possible after a game so that his notes and the game are still fresh in his mind. The head coach should trust his scout, and not question or doubt him if he remembers something different from the last time he saw the team play.

Scouting is an important addition to the game plan, but it is a flexible addition and must be kept in its proper perspective.

GAME OPERATIONS

We try to emphasize some basic items on the day we are playing a game. We will normally have three meetings involving the coaches and the players. The first is at the pre-game meal, which, if we are playing a night game, is at noon. We meet again approximately two and a half hours prior to the start of the game in order to partake of a nutritious drink called Sustagen. It is at this meeting that the coaches review the opposition with the players, position by position. We feel these meetings are important so that any questions relative to the game that night can be resolved, and so our players are convinced that they are going into that basketball game as well prepared as possible.

We meet again in the basketball locker room 45 minutes before the game starts. At this time our players must be dressed, taped, and ready to play. For 15 minutes prior to our team's taking the floor I, as coach, again review, with the aid of the blackboard, our game plan for that night. Offenses and defenses are discussed, situations explained, man to man assignments restated, and our offensive and defensive plans for that night re-emphasized. I say restated and re-emphasized because, in preparing for this game during the practice week, we have gone over all of these items on the floor. However, I like to get our club together 45 minutes before the game to rededicate ourselves to the proposition at hand: to defeat the opponent for that particular night.

We take the basketball floor one half hour before the game starts. We are paired up and shoot quickly (and, we hope, accurately) for 15 minutes; then we go into an eight minute two-ball short shot shooting drill. We stress that this drill be run at top speed by each of the players on the floor. We like to end our pre-game practice with this speedy drill in order to get us into the proper frame of mind for starting the game at 100 per cent ability when the tip-off goes at the proper time. During the course of the game we expect each of our players, whether called on to play at a particular time or in ready reserve, to be completely involved. The players on our bench should be active, excited, and watching their positions so that, if they are called on to play, they can step into the breach and do a good job immediately. Our players who are called on to start or to substitute are expected to expend every ounce of energy, if necessary.

During our practice sessions we try to drill poise into our club, since we feel very strongly that the well poised basketball team is going to be a winning basketball team. We do not allow our players to question the calls of either referee. We want nothing to put a chink in their armor of poise, as this self-control and self-discipline can actually be an important factor in winning or losing the game.

I chuckle when I think of a statement by Thomas Edison, who said that the greatest thinking is done in solitude, and the worst is done in confusion. Basketball coaches and players are required to make important decisions during the course of a game when anywhere from 5,000 to 20,000 fans are screaming at the top of their lungs, and noise and confusion reign. Nevertheless, the coach must be able to call on a high level of poise in order to make these decisions and, of course, his players must do the same thing.

On the high school or collegiate level, I do not think it beyond the realm of possibility for a player who is properly drilled and conditioned to play either 32 or 40 minutes of tough, competitive basketball. We want each of our players to understand that he may be called on to play. From the opening tip-off until the final whistle, I never want a player of mine to look at the bench, point to his stomach, and ask to be taken out of the game. As a coach, I am in complete charge of substitutions, and feel that any coach cognizant of what is going on is able to see if a player of his needs relief. The coach is the one responsible for time-outs, and he is the only one allowed to call a time-out at the University of Michigan.

During the course of the game I keep a close watch on the number of time-outs we have had, the number of personal fouls on our players, and the number of team fouls on each club. The score and the time are usually visible to me.

The coach is responsible for operating his team, and it is up to him to see that they perform to the very best of their ability. I re-emphasize the fact that teams are actually developed, conditioned, and become operational in practice. To try to accomplish this just during the course of the game is impossible.

The playing of the game is the culmination of many hours of work, both on and off the basketball floor, for both the players and the coach. It is important that everything be very well organized on this day, that the players know what is expected of them, and that everyone performs at the top of his ability.

Our players are expected to approach the game with seriousness of purpose, and with one idea in mind—to win!

BENCH CONDUCT—
PLAYERS AND COACH

It is important that each player be made to feel that he is an integral, important part of the team. With that thought in mind, we demand that every player be entirely involved with the game, whether he is physically playing or not. I want our players not on the floor to be eager, alert, and attentive to the action with the idea that they will be ready when called upon to play. We don't allow our players on the bench to sit back and relax, or to verbally harass officials or opposing players. We want them to be intent on the game, in particular the man or men they might be called upon to guard. The substitute is most important. We want him to feel important. The substitute has the difficult job of going into a game physically cold and being expected to fill the breach immediately. We want him mentally ready to do this.

Because of the disgraceful bench actions of a small minority of basket-ball coaches, the following NCAA rule is in the rulebook (Rule 10—Section 7) relative to the bench action of coaches and others: "A coach, substitute, team attendant, or follower shall not disrespectfully address or bait an Official or opponent; nor indicate his objection to an Official's decision by rising from the bench or using gestures; nor do anything to incite undesirable crowd reactions; nor shall he enter the court unless by permission of an Official to attend an injured player. Coaches shall remain seated on the bench except that while the clock is stopped they may leave the bench to direct or encourage players who are on the court. Coaches may, at any time, leave the bench to confer with substitutes, to signal players to request a time-out, or to perform other necessary coaching responsibilities. During an intermission or time-out charged to a team the coach and/or team attendants may confer with their players at or near their bench."

I understand and respect this rule, and I respect the officials and know that our sport is a tough one to officiate. However, basketball, as played today, is action packed, noisy, raucous, and tough, and to expect a coach responsible for one of the teams playing to sit quietly is unreasonable. Most coaches do not violate the spirit of this rule, but many, including myself, violate the letter of the rule.

The coach is paid to direct his team. I want my players to know that I am in that game with them all the way, and I want to show them by some type of physical encouragement as well as vocal help. I don't condone berating of officials, and feel that the coach who does this should be penalized. When I find myself sitting quietly and calmly on the bench when the game is in progress, either we have the game locked up or we're beaten.

The basketball coach has to be prepared to make command decisions (which could enable his team to win or lose) in the worst possible conditions, but he must make them, regardless of screaming crowds or noisy bands. Players properly expect the coach to come up with the right answers at the right time. The coach properly expects his players to execute his plans correctly, so he had better have the right answers. It's not easy, but it's part of the game.

JUMP BALLS

Possession of the basketball is of the utmost importance, and such details as how to maneuver a team to obtain possession of the ball on a ·toss must not be overlooked. The ball is tossed at least twice in the college game, four times in the high school game, and of course many more times in the normal course of the game.

We try and break our jump ball situations into three categories: offensive tap (which means we should control the tip), defensive tap (which means the opponent should control), and an even tap (when our chances are 50-50).

We will do the same thing on our jump ball in each given situation 90 per cent of the time. I don't like to say 100 per cent, because there can always be a peculiar quirk in the circumstances which could force us out of our prearranged and practiced plan.

Offensive Tap

In this situation we always like to tip forward and rotate right.

We tell X3 he must control the ball which X5 taps up and toward him. He must go after the ball, hard, grab it with both hands, and see if he can hit X4. He can also, in some circumstances, tap the ball back toward his offensive goal for X4. We do this if the opposition is not in a good defensive position, but are playing our team man for man. The third alternative is to tap the ball right back to X5, who must always be alert for the ball.

We use this offensive tip from any of the three jumping positions on the floor. We prefer to tap forward so that everybody on our team knows where the ball is going. X1 remains back as defensive safety valve. X2 remains in place as an alternate receiver, 10 per cent of the time; when the ball is tapped he explodes for the goal. X3 receives the ball and either hits X4, taps back to X5, or retains possession. X4 goes for the offensive goal. X5 taps the ball and stays set until he sees what is going on.

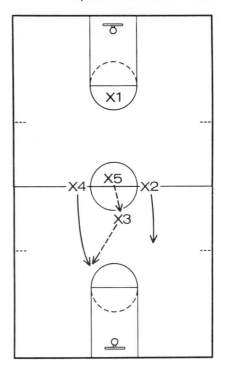

Defensive Tap—Center Court

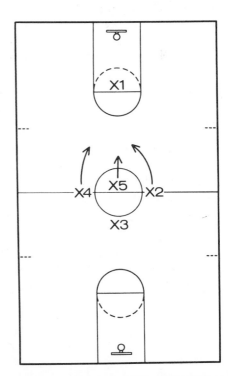

X1 is deep, defensive safety. X2 rotates to his right for defense. X3 remains in spot and looks for the ball. X4 remains in spot and then retreats toward goal when the ball is lost. X5 jumps and then retreats.

Defensive Tap—Defensive and Offensive Ends

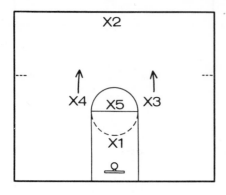

Offensive End.

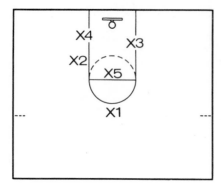

Defensive End.

Defensive End

X1 is at top of the circle. X3 and X4 are deep, defensively. X2 shades toward the basket and lines up on the side where the opposition has concentrated its power. We hope to steal the ball, but our primary objective is not to allow a cheap field goal from the tap.

Offensive End

X1 is offensively played to make the defense conscious. X5 tips forward and then retreats. X2 is deep safety valve man. X3 and X4 are defensively placed to try to stop the quick offensive thrust.

Even Tap—Center and Offensive End of Court

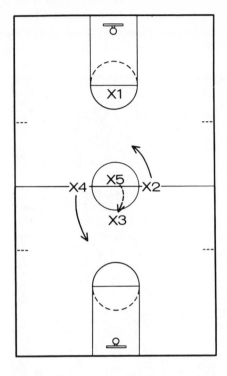

X5 jumps and taps forward. X1 remains deep as safety valve. X4 rotates to his right toward the offensive goal. X2 rotates to his right as defender.

Even Tap—Defensive End

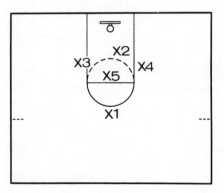

We play this as we would a defensive tap on the same position, i.e., cautiously and with the idea of stopping an easy basket.

Our idea on all jump balls is to try to cover every conceivable situation, leaving nothing open to chance, and therefore we prepare our team for these situations. We feel our rules are simple, understandable, and, if executed correctly, will prove successful.

Center Jump. Buntin of Michigan vs. Bradds of Ohio State.

Center Jump. Tison of Duke vs. Buntin of Michigan. Fouls do occur on jump balls.

Center Jump—Buntin, #22, of Michigan vs.
Brown of Princeton.

STATISTICS

The statistical side of any basketball game can, if viewed in the proper perspective by the coach and his team, paint a fairly accurate picture of what has transpired during the playing time. At Michigan we like to be cognizant of shooting percentages for both field goal and foul. The field goal percentages, when viewed in conjunction with an accurately kept shot chart, may give information as to the opposition's defense, and may give the coach some insight as to the efficiency of his offense.

The rebounding statistics also give vital information if accurately kept. These show who is, or who is not, carrying his weight on the backboards, and in my judgment the most important rebounding statistic is the one which emulates from the defensive board.

I personally view the turnover statistic, i.e., the number of times each club gives the ball up from its possession by means of other than a shot, as most important. This record may show the operating efficiency of a basketball team.

Personal fouls, of course, play an important part in any basketball game, and the coach has to have this information at hand during the course of a game so he can conduct the game and manipulate his personnel properly. I am against any rule change which would allow a player to continue in the game regardless of exceeding the five personal foul limit rule which is now in effect. This disqualification rule is unique to basketball, and it is a good one. The five foul rule does make the coach think and plan quite a bit, and that's what he is paid for.

The capable coach must guard against using statistics as a crutch or an excuse for losing. Statistics only reflect what has transpired. It is easy and tempting for the losing coach to grab the statistics and note, for example, that the other club shot 50 per cent and his team shot only 25 per cent, and then ask how anyone could beat a team that shot so well on that particular night. What statistics do not show is why one team shot so poorly and the other team so well. This is what the coach must determine.

We try to use our statistics in order to benefit from past performances, and improve our club individually and collectively. We place them in their proper perspective. Statistics cannot, by themselves, win or lose for a coach, but the coach who handles them correctly can aid his club's operating efficiency.

PRE-SEASON CONDITIONING

The NCAA rule on pre-season practice, which reads, "pre-season practice in basketball shall not begin prior to October Fifteenth of each year," prohibits us from any type of organized work prior to that time. We abide by this rule, naturally, and do nothing on an organized basis with our basketball players.

Our team knows that we expect them to report on October Fifteenth in some semblance of good physical condition, as we like to use our six weeks prior to the opening game on developing team play and fundamentals, and not on just conditioning. During the period of time from the beginning of school until October 15 we recommend the following types of exercises for our basketball hopefuls:

1. Since basketball is a game of short sprints, we recommend that our team work on this type of activity. Many will work out with our track team, and we like to have them sprint the straightaways and walk the curves. Each player determines when and in how much of this activity he will participate. I do not believe that cross-country work adds to the physical conditioning which is so important in basketball. I personally never recommend any type of running that is at less than full speed. This goes back to our original prem-

ise that basketball is a game of habits, and we want to instill the correct ones.

2. We recommend for leg and lung conditioning that they spend some time sprinting up and down the stadium steps, starting at the first row and running up to the top. We have weighted vests available which we encourage them to wear in order to expedite this conditioning program.

3. After my first three years of coaching, the lifting of weights was eliminated from our pre-season conditioning program. I don't know if this was because I had begun to think that it was incompatible to suggest weight-lifting while trying to stress the development of a soft and delicate shooting touch, or if the advent of such big, strong players as Bill Buntin, Cazzie Russell, and Oliver Darden made me think that weight-lifting seemed a little useless.

4. Although we don't control in any way a boy's play on the intramural court, I recommend to my Varsity aspirants that they refrain from any type of two on two, three on three basketball starting from the first of October. Although much can be accomplished in this type of basketball physical activity, unsupervised play can also result in injuries which could deprive your team of some of its better talent.

In informal discussions with our boys prior to the beginning of practice, we emphasize just one thing to them: when practice starts we expect them to be physically ready to begin.

DISCIPLINE

Participation in a high school or collegiate basketball team is a privilege restricted to very few young men, and these young men must understand that in order to earn this right they must become disciplined people, mentally and physically.

Participation in any interscholastic or intercollegiate athletic team is an extracurricular activity which is neither required nor expected of all students. The student who chooses to compete does so of his own free will, and it can be expected that he will conform to a different set of rules and regulations than does the average student.

As has been mentioned, we have a set of terms which specify the way in which we expect our team members to conduct themselves. Our terms state that there will be no smoking or drinking, that the player will attend all classes and make an honest academic effort, that he will present a neat appearance both on campus and on the road, that he will attend all practices and be punctual for such, and shall conduct himself as a good citizen at all times so that he will be a fine representative of his university.

We've been asked what should be done if parents or the school allow some things which these rules forbid. Admittedly, at the college level we do not have the same relationship with parents as the high school coach has. However, my answer would be that, since athletics are an extracurricular activity and non-compulsory, these terms, or rules, must be observed. There can be no exceptions.

The crux of discipline is not in the rules or regulations, but in their administration. Every coach and player hopes to avoid disciplinary problems, but these problems continue to appear, and they must be handled efficiently and with dispatch. There is no easy way to deal with this important area of discipline. The guideposts and points of emphasis which we use are as follows:

1. We emphasize the word respect—respect of player for coach, of coach for player, and of player for player. Without this firm foundation of interwoven respect the team's chances of success are slim.
2. Everyone connected with the team has a knowledge of the terms, and knows what is correct or incorrect. The coaching staff does not play policeman, but the squad must be aware that any indiscretion on their part will be reported to the coach. This is the nature of the game.
3. Each disciplinary case must be judged by the coach on its own merits; the coach is judge and jury. I do not think that the team members should be given the facts or asked for their opinion. This is the responsibility of the head coach, and the coach who gives it to his team is shirking his duty. The player who violates the covenant does in effect betray both his coaches and teammates, but the disciplinary action should be taken by the coach.

    John McClendon, the fine coach at Cleveland State, had a unique system for taking disciplinary action. He went to his team, stated that so and so had misused their trust, and could be reinstated if he ran three miles in under 20 minutes, and if *every other member* of the team also ran the three miles. I've never used this, but I'm sure it has merit.
4. Every player must be treated the same. There can be no preferential treatment shown, regardless of the player's ability. If a coach commits the cardinal sin of playing a favorite or two, he and his club are destined for failure. I know it is difficult to arrive at a harsh but fair decision which could suspend, for example, your most productive player, but if he deserves the punishment then punish him, and both the coach and his squad will be much better off.
5. The players should know that the coach will keep their confidence. I do not think that the reasons for disciplinary actions are public domain. This is no one's business but the parties immediately concerned.
6. The types of action which can be taken are varied, and can include such things as permanent suspension, suspension for the season, for a number of games or a game, suspension from practice, or extra punishing physical work. The important thing is to have the punishment fit the crime. Be firm in the

knowledge that you, as coach, have all the facts before you and are being fair, make the correct decision, and never second guess yourself.

In my judgment, the average player of high school or college age does respect authority and does need and desire a fair set of terms to follow; he expects to be guided firmly and fairly.

INTERNATIONAL BASKETBALL

During the month of August, 1965, eleven members of the University of Michigan basketball team, plus two coaches and an official, made a good will tour of the Middle East. Our team was chosen to make this trip upon recommendation of the United States Basketball Federation, and we were sponsored by the United States State Department, Department of Cultural Presentations. During this trip we visited four countries, Egypt, Turkey, Algeria, and Greece, performed in a dozen cities, played seven competitive games, and conducted approximately 15 clinics. We were the guests of the basketball federations of these four countries.

We found the trip most interesting and enjoyable, and I would like to give some of my observations of basketball as it is played in that part of the world.

In Egypt we found the reception for our team extremely enthusiastic. We played in front of crowds which ranged from 3,000 to 6,000, and in my judgment the caliber of play of the Egyptians was good. Since we were sponsored by the Basketball Federation of the United States, we were not allowed to play teams at a national team level, therefore our competition was made up of club teams. There were on these club teams, however, many players who also competed on the national teams, so the level of competition was fairly high.

In Egypt we played in the only indoor court we were to see on our trip. Every other basketball court in the countries we visited was outdoors and consisted of a clay or blacktop surface. Alexandria had a gymnasium which seated about 6,000 people, and this was the only place in which we played that was comparable to any facility that we have in the United States.

In Turkey we played in Istanbul and Uskadar, and competed against college age students who were going to play in the World Student Games in Budapest later in August. We played only one competitive game in Turkey, but our coaches and players worked individually and collectively with this Turkish team. Our team was again very well received by the Turkish people, and the crowds before which we played were enthusiastic and very kind to the boys on our team.

From Turkey we journeyed to Greece, and played two competitive games in this country. In Thessalonica we played against a very good Greek team in front of an enthusiastic crowd of 4,000, and we won by some seven points. The next day we flew back to Athens in preparation for a game the following night against the champion club team of Greece. This game was played in the stadium which held the first modern Olympiad in 1896. The court was placed in the infield, and a crowd of some 12,000 came to watch the game. This audience was like the crowds we run into in places like Bloomington, Indiana, East Lansing, Michigan, and Champaign, Illinois, in that they knew for whom they were rooting and were quite vociferous in their support. As I mentioned earlier, we had an American official with us, and he became the target of quite a bit of abuse in this particular game. From what I was able to gather, in international rules the offensive man can do no wrong. Consequently, in this game, when our official called some offensive charging fouls, which I thought were legitimate, the crowd reacted, along with their coach and players, in quite a vocal manner. This game was fairly close throughout, and with approximately two minutes to play our referee called a charging foul on their best player, which was his fifth and disqualified him. At this point the crowd became most angry and some even charged our referee. Frankly, I was concerned for his safety, as well as our own. Our captain, Larry Tregoning, a great player and a fierce competitor, said, "Coach, let's blow this game and get the hell out of here. I'm supposed to get married next week and I'd like to be there." I was inclined to agree with him, but we finished the game, which at the close was tied 81-81. Under international rules an overtime period of five minutes is called for, with the teams changing baskets. With Greece's best player out, our chances of surviving looked fairly good, but their coach said, through his interpreter, that they weren't going to play any more because our referee was unfair. There was nothing we could do about this situation. However, our team did take its position on the court and made the Greek team leave the court before we did. I don't think we upset Greek-United States relationships too much, and this sort of treatment reminded us of home.

The final stop in our trip was in Algeria, where our team performed in the cities of Algiers, Ténès, and Cherchel. The Algerian national team had just returned from the African Games and had finished a disappointing last; consequently, their enthusiasm for basketball was at a low ebb. We found that in this country, although the interest in basketball was quite a bit less than in the other countries, their national coach and the people in the federation were most anxious for improvement.

I feel this trip was a worthwhile venture, and that our American boys benefited a great deal from being exposed to basketball in these countries. The fans and people in general in these countries were impressed with basketball in the United States, because of the caliber of play as well as the fine young men on our team. I was personally very much impressed with the young American Cultural and Public Affairs Officers connected with the United States Information Service who did everything possible to aid us, and who are doing an excellent job for the United States—such men as Sam Courtney in Istanbul, Bob Wozniak in Athens, and Harold Brazil in Cairo. There is also a great deal of logistical work and planning involved in sending a team such as ours to these countries, and I was much impressed by the way our trip was handled in Washington by such people as Nick Rodis and Al Smith in the Cultural Affairs Office.

The conclusions to which I came upon the completion of our trip concerning basketball in Europe and Africa are as follows:

1. *Players.* It seems to me that their forte is in ball handling—passing, receiving, and dribbling—and that they do this very well. Perhaps the nature of the basketball rules under which they play emphasize this, but it appeared to me that the players in these countries overemphasize this part of the game, and consequently their shooting suffers. The glaring weakness, when comparing these players with the American boys, is that our young men can shoot the basketball from 10 to 25 feet with much greater accuracy than could anyone against whom we played. The players and teams exhibited great *esprit de corps;* all seemed to take great pride in their performances. The number of boys participating in basketball, percentagewise, is much less than we have in our country. It astonished many of the people with whom we came in contact when we told them we were just one of many college or amateur teams in this country.

2. *Coaches.* We met the coach of the national team in every country we visited, and found these men to be learned and educated people who were eager for knowledge relative to the game of basketball. Coaching was an avocation, not a vocation, for these men. Each deemed it a great honor to be the coach of their respective national teams. I feel that under the guidance of men such as these basketball in these countries can only be improved. One of the coaches made an interesting point when he stated that he felt playing against teams such as ours benefited them a great deal, and that the United States did a great deal to improve the caliber of the Russian basketball team by playing them each year. In his opinion, our country, by engaging in this yearly competition with the Russians, was making it possible for the Russian team to be dominant in Europe.

3. *Facilities.* We found the facilities in each country to be very marginal at best by our standards. As mentioned previously, we played only one game indoors, in Alexandria. The other courts were outdoors, and made of either clay, concrete, or asphalt. The players' personal equipment—shoes, uni-

forms, and so on—was in short supply, as was the supply of basketballs. The dominant type of basketball used was rubber, dictated by the fact of playing outside.

4. *Fans.* We found the fans to be generally enthusiastic, particularly in Egypt and Greece. They resembled our fans in that they were fairly knowledgeable and vocal, and seemed to enjoy the game a great deal.

5. *Rules.* In my judgment, the International Olympic Rules are not as logical as the American rules, but perhaps this is because I am more familiar with the rules as we know them in the United States.

Major Differences

1. *Back Court—Front Court*

   There is *no* front court or back court. The floor is *not* divided into two areas.

2. *#86: Thirty Second Rule*

   (a) After gaining possession a team must try for goal within 30 seconds. Failure to do so means loss of ball and throw in by opponents at side line nearest to where violation occurred.

   (b) Team control continues (30 second count continues) until a try for goal, ball becomes dead, or opponent secures control.

   (c) If a player deliberately throws or bats ball into an opponent, causing it to go out of bounds, the ball shall be awarded to opponent.

3. *#13b: Thirty Second Clock*

   A suitable device, visible to players and spectators, shall be provided for the administration of the 30 second rule and shall be operated by a 30 second operator.

4. *#93: Fouls in Act of Shooting*

   If a player is fouled in the act of trying for a goal and the try is successful, *no* free throw is awarded unless foul is intentional (if intentional, one free throw is awarded). In other words, there is no such thing as our three point play. The offending player is charged with a foul. If the field goal attempt is missed, two free throws are awarded. If no free throw penalty is awarded as result of a foul in act of shooting, the officials shall signal to the scorer the number of offending player, and *hand* the ball to the thrower from *behind the end line.*

5. *#93: Personal Fouls* (not in act of shooting)

   When a player commits a personal foul, except in the act of shooting, no free throw shall be awarded. Charge foul to offending player. Ball put in play on sideline nearest foul.

6. *#93: Fouls in Last Five Minutes*

   During the last five minutes of second half and during all extra periods, *all* personal fouls shall be considered as committed on a player who is throwing for goal—all are two shot penalties.

7. *#57: Clock Stops Every Time Whistle Blows in Last Five Minutes*
   During the last five minutes of play of the second half and all extra periods, the clock will stop every time the official blows his whistle.

8. *#91: Technical Foul by Player*
   Penalty is two free throws. Players line up along lanes and ball remains in play after second free throw.

9. *#92: Technical Foul by Coach or Substitute*
   Penalty is one free throw. Ball awarded out of bounds at mid-court to offended team, as in NCAA rules.

10. *#71: Putting Ball in Play from Out of Bounds*
    Ball is put in play at *sideline* nearest spot of violation. *No* out of bounds at end line.

11. *#85: Three Second Rule*
    The count starts the moment the thrower-in has possession of the ball. In force on all out of bounds situations.

12. *#7: Free Throw Lanes*
    The lane to lane distance on base line is 19 feet, ⅜ inches. In other words, approximately 3½ feet wider along base line on each side of the lane than NCAA rules.

Other Differences

1. *#14: Officials Exchange Positions*
   After each foul involving a free throw penalty and each *jump* ball, the officials shall exchange positions.

2. *#21: Simultaneous Decisions*
   If officials make simultaneous decisions on same play and violations involve different penalties, the *more severe* penalty is imposed.

3. *#24: Disagreement in Score Sheet*
   When there is disagreement in score sheet between running score and individual scoring, the *individual scoring shall count.*

4. *#29: Substitutes After Successful Free Throw*
   Only the player who has attempted the free throw may be substituted.

5. *#56: Overtime Periods*
   Five minute overtime periods with two minutes between overtime periods. Toss of coin is made to determine choice of baskets for first overtime period. Teams change baskets for each successive overtime period.

6. *#58: Coach May Request Time-out*
   The coach may request time-out by *notifying scorer* personally, or by using mechanical device, if available.

7. *#60: Two Legal Charged Time-outs per Half*
   Each team may be granted no more than *two time-outs* per half, and no more than one for each overtime period. Time-outs *may not* be accumulated.

8. *#76: Five Seconds Allowed for Free Throw*
   Five seconds is maximum time allowed for free throw try once ball has been placed at disposal of free thrower.
9. *#79: Violation of Free Throw Provision*
   If violation of breaking plane of lane is by a teammate of free thrower and free throw is successful, the goal shall count and violation is disregarded. Only the free thrower can nullify a successful free throw by a lane violation—not his teammate.
10. *#80: Force-out Rule*
    Official may award ball out of bounds to player in possession who is forced out of bounds by negligent contact.
11. *#100: Five Foul Disqualification—Technical or Personal*
    A total of five fouls (either technical or personal) shall disqualify a player.
12. *#20: Substitute to Shoot Free Throw for Injured Player*
    If injured player cannot resume play in one minute, only his substitute may shoot the free throw.
13. *#24: Scorer to Notify Coach of Time-outs*
    The scorer, through the official, *shall* notify the coach when he has taken a second time-out in each half.
14. *#28: Only Captain May Address Official*
    The designated captain is the only one who may address the official on matters of interpretation, if done in a cautious matter.
15. *#29 and #32: Substitutes and Uniform Numbers*
    Each team shall be allowed no more than seven substitutes. The uniform numbers shall be from four to fifteen.
16. *#29: Substitution Time Limited to 20 Seconds*
    If more than 20 seconds is used in substitution, a time-out shall be charged.
17. *#54: Ten Minute Intermission at Half-time*
    The game is played in two 20 minute halves with ten minutes between halves.
18. *#65: Jumpers Must Have Both Feet Inside Circle*
    The two jumpers shall stand with *both* feet inside the circle prior to the toss for a jump ball.
19. *#77: All Periods Must Start with Jump Ball*
    Regardless of when a technical foul is called, all periods must start with a jump ball at center.
20. *#94 and #97b: Double Fouls and False Double Fouls*
    Play is resumed following a double foul or false double foul by a jump ball at *nearest* circle—not at mid-court.

I would agree with Hank Iba, who coached the United States Olympic team, when he said that the United States cannot expect to continue to win every basketball game they play in Olympic competition. Although this country is still the leader in development of skillful basketball players, other countries are making great improvements. Their basketball people have a great thirst for knowledge and are very industrious, and the combination of these things will make for continued improvement. Also, the fact that many of these foreign teams are being exposed to United States players is going to have a profound, positive effect on their play.

SPECTATORS, RULES, TERMINOLOGY

Basketball is a great spectator sport, watched by more people than any other sport played in America. It seems to me that the spectator should learn some aspects of the game so that he can enjoy the games more. Few people know the exact dimensions of the playing courts, or the dimensions, sizes, and materials of the backboards, baskets, and basketballs. Some knowledge of the rules seems to be in order for the fan to know what's going on in the game.

The following definitions and rules were taken from the Official Basketball Rules as adopted by the National Basketball Committee of the United States. The complete entries are not shown here. I have made some additions and deletions and have edited these phrases to make them simple to understand.

The Game

Basketball is played by two teams of five players each. The purpose of each team is to throw the ball into its own basket and prevent the other team from scoring. The ball may be thrown, batted, rolled, or dribbled in any direction, subject to restrictions laid down in the following rules.

The Court Dimensions

The playing court shall be a rectangular surface free from obstructions and with dimensions not greater than 94 feet in length by 50 feet in width. Ideal measurements are:

High School Age .... 50 by 84 feet
College Age .... 50 by 94 feet

Equipment

Each of the two backboards shall be of any rigid material. The front surface shall be flat and, unless it is transparent, it shall be white. The backboard shall be one of two types: (1) a rectangle six feet horizontally and four feet vertically, or (2) a fan-shaped backboard.

The Ball, Specifications, Color

The ball shall be spherical. Its color shall be the approved orange shade or natural tan. For college games, it shall have a leather cover unless the teams agree to use a ball with a composition cover. For high school or YMCA games, it shall have a leather or composition cover. It shall be of the molded type. If the panels are leather, they shall be cemented to the spherically molded fabric which surrounds an air-tight rubber lining. Its circumference shall be within a maximum of 30 inches and a minimum of 29½ inches for adults and within a maximum of 29½ inches and a minimum of 29 inches for players below senior high school age. Its weight shall be not less than 20 nor more than 22 ounces. It shall be inflated to an air pressure such that when it is dropped to a solid wood floor from a height of six feet, measured to the bottom of the ball, it will rebound to a height, measured to the top of the ball, of not less than 49 inches when it strikes on its least resilient spot, nor more than 54 inches when it strikes on its most resilient spot.

Backboards—Positions

Each backboard shall be midway between the sidelines, with the plane of its front face perpendicular to the floor, parallel to the end line and four feet from it. The upper edge of the backboard shall be 13 feet above the floor for the rectangular and 12 feet 8 inches for the fan shaped backboard. The backboards shall be protected from spectators to a distance of at least three feet at each end.

Baskets—Size, Material

Each basket shall consist of a metal ring, 18 inches in inside diameter, its flange and braces, and a white cord 12-mesh net, 15 to 18 inches in length, suspended from beneath the ring.

The Referee—Duties

The referee shall inspect and approve all equipment, including court, baskets, ball, backboards, and timers' and scorers' signals. Prior to the scheduled starting time of the game, he shall designate the official time-piece, its operator, the official scorebook, and official scorer. He shall not permit any player to wear equipment which in his judgment is dangerous to other players or is unnatural and designed to increase height or to gain a similar advantage. He shall be responsible for notifying each captain three minutes before each half is to begin.

The referee shall toss the ball at center to start the game. He shall decide whether a goal shall count if the officials disagree. He shall have power to forfeit a game when conditions warrant. He shall decide matters upon which the timers and the scorers disagree. At the end of each half he shall check and approve the score. His approval at the end of the game terminates the jurisdiction of the officials. Neither official shall have the authority to set aside or question decisions made by the other within the limits of his respective outlined duties.

Behavior of Spectators

The home management or game committee, insofar as they can reasonably be expected to exercise control, is responsible for the behavior of spectators. The officials may call fouls on either team if its supporters act in such a way as to interfere with proper conduct of the game. Discretion must be used in calling such fouls, however, lest a team be unjustly penalized.

Basket

A basket is the 18-inch ring, its flanges, braces, and appended net, through which players attempt to throw the ball. A team's own basket is the one into which its players try to throw the ball. The visiting team shall have the irrevocable choice of baskets at which it may practice before the game, and this basket shall be its choice for the first half. The teams shall change baskets for the second half.

In Control—Player, Team

A player is in control when he is holding a live ball or dribbling it. A team is in control when a player of the team is in control and also while a live ball is being passed between teammates. Team control continues until there is a try for the goal, an opponent secures control, or the ball becomes dead. There is no team control during a jump ball, a throw in, a try for goal, or during the tapping of a rebound. In these situations, team control is re-established when a player secures control.

Disqualified Player

A disqualified player is one who is barred from further participation in the game because of committing his fifth personal foul, or a flagrant foul.

Dribble

A dribble is ball movement caused by a player in control who throws or taps the ball in the air or onto the floor and then touches it once or several times or catches it. The dribble ends when the dribbler: (a) touches the ball with both hands simultaneously, or (b) permits it to come to rest while he is in contact with it, or (c) loses control of it. An air-dribble is that part of a dribble during which the dribbler throws or taps the ball in the air and then touches it before it touches the floor.

Extra Period

Extra period is the extension of playing time necessary to break a tie score.

Foul

A foul is an infraction of the rules, the penalty for which is one or more free throws, unless it is a double foul or a player control foul, in which case the free throw provision is canceled. For convenience, a personal foul which is neither flagrant, intentional, committed against a player trying for field goal, nor a part of a double or multiple foul is termed a common foul.

Double Foul

A double foul is a situation in which two opponents commit personal fouls against each other at approximately the same time. A false double foul is a situation in which there are fouls by both teams, the second of which occurs before the clock is started following the first, but such that at least one of the attributes of a double foul is absent.

Multiple Foul

A multiple foul is a situation in which two or more teammates commit personal fouls against the same opponent at approximately the same time. A false multiple foul is a situation in which there are two or more fouls by the same team and such that the last foul is committed before the clock is started following the first, and such that at least one of the attributes of a multiple foul is absent.

Personal Foul

A personal foul is a player foul which involves contact with an opponent while the ball is alive or after the ball is in possession of a player for a throw-in.

Player Control Foul

A player control foul is a common foul committed by a player while he or a teammate is in control.

Technical Foul

A technical foul is a foul by a nonplayer or a player foul which does not involve contact with an opponent, or a player foul which involves unsportsmanlike contact with an opponent while the ball is dead.

Free Throw

A free throw is the privilege given a player to score one point by an unhindered try for goal from within the free throw circle and behind the free throw line. A free throw starts when the ball is given to the free thrower at the free throw line or is placed on the line. It ends when the try is successful, or it is certain the try will not be successful, or when the try touches the floor or any player, or when the ball becomes dead.

Front and Back Court

A team's front court consists of that part of the court between its end line and the nearer edge of the division line, and includes its basket and the inbounds part of its backboard. A team's back court consists of the rest of the court, including its opponent's basket, inbounds part of the backboard, and the entire division line.

Live Ball

A live ball is in the front or back court of the team in control as follows: (1) A ball which is in contact with a player or with the court is in the back court if either the ball or the player (either player if the ball is touching more than one) is touching the back court. It is in the front court if neither the ball nor the player is touching the back court; (2) A ball which is not in contact with a player or the court retains the same status as when it was last in contact with a player or the court.

Held Ball

Held ball occurs when two opponents have one or both hands so firmly on the ball that neither can gain possession without undue roughness. Held ball in the front court also occurs after five seconds during which (1) A closely guarded player, in an attempt to consume time, dribbles and/or holds the ball in his mid-court area or within a few feet of a boundary intersection; or (2) A closely guarded player anywhere in his front court holds the ball and is unable to pass or try for goal, or is withholding the ball from play; or (3) A team controls the ball in an area enclosed by screening teammates. The player in control is closely guarded when his opponent is in guarding stance at a distance not exceeding six feet from him.

Jump Ball

A jump ball is a method of putting the ball into play by tossing it up between two opponents in one of the three circles.

Location of a Player

The location of a player (or nonplayer) is determined by where he is touching the floor as far as being inbounds, out of bounds, in the front court, or back court is concerned. When he is in the air from a leap, his status with reference to these two factors is the same as at the time he was last in contact with the floor or an extension of the floor such as a bleacher. When the ball touches an official it is the same as touching the floor at the official's location.

Mid-court Area

The mid-court area of a team is that part of its front court between the division line and a parallel imaginary line approximately three feet outside that part of the free throw circle which is farthest from the end line.

Multiple Throw

A multiple throw is a succession of free throws attempted by the same team.

Pass

A pass is movement of the ball caused by a player who throws, bats, or rolls the ball to another player.

Penalty

A penalty for a foul is the charging of the offender with the foul and awarding one or more free throws or awarding the ball to the opponents for a throw-in. The penalty for a violation is the awarding of the ball to the opponents for a throw-in or one or more points or a substitute free throw.

Pivot

A pivot takes place when a player who is holding the ball steps once or more than once in any direction with the same foot, the other foot, called the pivot foot, being kept at its point of contact with the floor.

Traveling

Running with the ball (traveling) is moving a foot or the feet in any direction in excess of prescribed limits while holding the ball. The limits follow: (1) A player who receives the ball while standing still may pivot, using either foot as the pivot foot; (2) A player who receives the ball while his feet are moving or who is dribbling may stop as follows: (a) If he catches the ball while *both feet* are off the floor and: (1) *He alights with both feet* touching the floor simultaneously, he may pivot using either foot as the pivot foot; or (2) *He alights with first one foot* touching the floor followed by the other, he may pivot using the first foot to touch the floor as the pivot foot; or (3) *He alights on one foot*, he may jump off that foot and alight with both feet simultaneously, but he may not pivot before releasing the ball; (b) If he catches the ball while only *one foot* is off the floor: (1) He may step with the foot which is off the floor and may then pivot using the other foot as the pivot foot, or (2) *He may jump* with the foot which is on the floor and alight with both feet simultaneously, but he may not pivot before releasing the ball.

Try for Field Goal

A try for field goal is an attempt by a player to score two points by throwing the ball into his basket. The try starts when the player begins the motion which habitually precedes actual throw. The try ends when the throw is successful, or it is certain the throw will not be successful, or when the thrown ball touches the floor or any player, or when the ball becomes dead. The thrower continues to be a thrower until the ball is clearly in flight.

Basket Interference and Goal Tending

No player may (a) touch the ball or basket when the ball is on or within either basket; nor touch the ball when it (b) is touching the cylinder having the ring as its lower base; or (c) is not touching the cylinder but is in downward flight during a try for field goal while the entire ball is above the basket ring level and before the ball has touched the ring or the try has ended.

Exception: In (a.) or (b), if a player near his own basket has his hand legally in contact with the ball, it is not a violation if his contact with the ball continues after it enters the cylinder, or if, in such action, he touches the basket.

Penalty: If violation is at the opponent's basket, offended team is awarded one point if during a free throw and two points in any other case. The crediting of the score and subsequent procedure are the same as if the awarded score had resulted from the ball having gone through the basket, except that the official shall hand the ball to a player of the team entitled to the throw-in. If violation is at a team's own basket, no points can be scored and the ball is awarded to the offended team at the out of bounds spot on the side at either end of the free throw line extended. If there is a violation by both teams, play shall be resumed by a jump ball between any two opponents in the nearest circle.

Three-Second Rule

No offensive player may remain for more than three seconds in that part of his free throw lane between the end line and the farther edge of the free throw line while the ball is in control of his team. Allowance shall be made for a player who, having been in the restricted area for less than three seconds, dribbles in to try for goal.

In addition to the specific rule book information and definitions, the knowledgeable spectator must be aware of basketball terminology and nomenclature. The impact of radio and television has brought a new concept of terminology relative to sporting events. For example, the football fan, in order to understand the sportscasters and writers, must know the meaning of such terms as blitz, bombs, stunts, draws, red dogs, and mad dogs. He's got to know the differences among tight ends, split ends, lonesome ends, set backs, flanker backs, corner backs, fearsome foursomes, monsters, left, right, roving, and many other terms. It appears that we're reaching a point where the naming of a player, move, or action is becoming more important than the player, move, or action itself. Basketball has not reached the same peak of terminology as football, but we're getting close! In order to understand explanations of coaches, radio and television announcers, or public address systems, the following definitions are given.

Basketball Nomenclature—Definitions

1. Guard—backcourt man or quarterback.
2. Forward—corner man or wing man.
3. Center—post man or pivot man.
4. Base line—end line which is 50 feet in length, four feet from the backboard (college floor), and runs parallel to the board.
5. Side line—94 feet in length and perpendicular to the end line. Runs on both sides of court.
6. Keyhole area—area bounded by foul line, end line, and sides of free throw area, 12 feet across and 19 feet from foul line to end line, 15 feet from foul line to basket. Called keyhole area when we had only six feet in width rather than 12 feet, hence the area resembled a keyhole.
7. Buffer zone—one foot area between defensive and offensive man on foul line when a foul is shot.
8. Three second area—keyhole area. No offensive player may be in this area more than three seconds with or without the ball.
9. Ten second line—line at mid-court, separating front and back courts and offensive and defensive ends of the floor.
10. Weak side—at the offensive end of the court, it signifies the side of the floor on which the ball is *not* located.
11. Strong side—this designates the side of the floor on which the offensive team has the ball at any given moment.
12. High post area—area above the foul line and bound by the foul circle.
13. Low post area—area below foul line and bound by the foul lines.

14. Man to man defense—each man, defensively, is assigned a particular person to guard.
15. Zone defense—defensive men are assigned zones to cover rather than men.
16. Pressure defense—close harassing, pestering type of defense. This may be either man to man pressure or zone pressure, and it may be pressure at half court, full court, or three-quarter court.
17. Single Post—offensive formation in which one man stations himself at either the high or low post.
18. Double post—two men are at the post position, one high and one low, or both low in tandem.
19. Open post—no offensive player is at either the high or low post.
20. Error or turnover—this occurs when the offense gives up the ball without a shot.
21. Disciplined offense—the coach has all the moves pre-planned.
22. Freelance offense—catch as catch can offense; alley ball.
23. Vertical moves—guard to forward direction.
24. Lateral moves—side to side moves; guard to guard moves.
25. Combination defense—defense which switches from a man to man to a zone or vice versa. Switches from defense to defense are determined by the offensive man.

The basketball spectator, by understanding the various terms and definitions, can enjoy the game more. The coach who must speak publicly to laymen, spectators, and newsmen would be wise to make sure that his listening audience is fully cognizant of the message he is delivering. I'm sure there are many other descriptive terms relative to basketball, but these are some which are used most often.

CHAPTER 7

Personal Conclusions

This book is a result of my 18 years of coaching, 11 years as an assistant coach at the University of Michigan, one year as head basketball coach at Idaho, and seven years as head basketball coach at Michigan. In the seven years of competing in the Big Ten our Michigan teams have finished tenth, eighth, fourth, and have won three championships. In my 11 years as an assistant coach our teams finished second, third, fifth, twice sixth, seventh, eighth, and four times ninth. The one year that I was at Idaho our team won 11 and lost 15 games. As you can see I have been associated with both winning and losing teams (believe me, if you've got a choice, take the winning).

I have been very fortunate as a head basketball coach. At the University of Idaho little was expected of a new, incoming coach when I took the job, but we did have some tough players who played very well. Although our record was not outstanding, we seemed to satisfy everyone. When the opportunity presented itself for me to return to Michigan, I took the job with full knowledge of what the basketball situation was at that particular time. The previous season Michigan had finished tenth in the Big Ten, and there was no help in sight; since I had been a part of the program I knew this. In other words, I was appointed basketball coach there with no place to go but up, and that was a good situation. Michigan was ripe for success in basketball, since there had been some down years, and there seemed no reason why a good high school player could not be recruited to play for Michigan.

I personally received excellent cooperation from all of the personnel at the university and was given the opportunity to hire two full-time assistants. I chose Jim Skala and Tom Jorgensen, both former Michigan captains, knowledgeable of the situation at Michigan, personal friends of mine who I knew would be loyal to the program, and, perhaps most important, both knew what we had to do to succeed. We attacked the job with the idea of not just doing our best, but of getting the job done. First we decided that we could be successful, and perhaps with some unrealistic enthusiasm eliminated the idea of failure. We felt we had a lot of plus factors on our side, first of which was that we were representing a great university that had worldwide academic status and a great athletic tradition.

Second, we had three full-time coaches who knew that good players were the life blood of any successful athletic program, and therefore decided to recruit very diligently and enthusiastically. We decided to recruit only boys we thought could make us winners. In other words, we made up our minds to take only boys we had actually seen play exciting basketball in high school.

Third, we had many good friends, including alumni of the university, who were working to help us in any way they could. Fourth, the Michigan State High School basketball program was, and has been, improving, and was in a position to produce high caliber players.

We were too late the first year to implement our program a great deal, as I was not hired until early June. We did recruit two tough little players, Bob Cantrell and Doug Herner, both 5' 10" back court men who had been rejected by some schools because of their size. They proved to be winners, playing on our eighth, fourth, and first place teams.

In our first full season we finished tenth, with a 6-18 over-all record and a 2-12 Big Ten record. In the spring of 1961, our first full recruiting year, we recruited Larry Tregoning and George Pomey, All-State players from Michigan and Illinois, respectively, and landed Bill Buntin, a young Detroiter who had been out of high school a year and was virtually unknown by college recruiters as he had broken his leg during the first game of his senior year in high school. Bill came to Michigan and became an All-American, three time All-Conference selection, and was the great center which all championship teams need.

The next spring, when the three aforementioned boys were freshmen, we had a real bonanza year in recruiting. Oliver Darden, 6' 7", from Detroit, enrolled at Michigan. Jim Myers, 6' 8", All-Stater from Ohio, chose Michigan for its Engineering School. John Clawson and John Thompson, two fine Illinois prospects, decided to cast their lots in Ann Arbor. And the biggest prize of all, a young man who was later to become a three time All-American and the nation's best collegiate player, Cazzie Russell, decided his future would be best at the University of Michigan.

These two classes of basketball players, 1962-63, combined their talents with great enthusiasm and industry, and led Michigan to three consecutive Big Ten Championships, two Mid-East Regional Championships, and a third and second place in the NCAA final competition. They were also judged first in the nation in the final UPI and AP polls in 1965. The only honor, and a big one, that escaped this group was the winning of the national championship. However, we did make the finals twice, but were defeated by Duke in the semi-final game in 1964, and by UCLA in the final game in 1965.

The success that our basketball teams have had in the past has spotlighted the need for a new and bigger arena, and one is now under construction in Ann Arbor, which, when completed, will be one of the finest in the country.

The resurgence of Michigan basketball has been due to the great talent, enthusiasm, and industry inherent in the group of young men I have just mentioned. It is perhaps easier to arrive at the top from the position from which we started than to remain there, but our big job now is to continue in the winning tradition.

I feel that it is a privilege to be a basketball coach, and that the coaching profession is a great and honorable one. Success in this profession, as in any profession, is a result of diligent, industrious work on the coach's part. Luck has very little to do with success in coaching. As someone once said, "Success is a matter of luck; just ask any failure."

There is no easy road to victory. There are many formations, both offensively and defensively, and some of these must be more effective than others. It is, however, my honest opinion that none of these movements by themselves will ever guarantee victory.

In many instances the coach makes a grievous error in overcoaching his team. Tony Hinkle, the great coach at Butler University, whose advice I sought when I received my first head coaching assignment, said that basketball is a very simple game; the idea is to put the ball in your basket and prevent your opponent from putting the ball in his.

There are no secrets to this game. The true secret of successful coaching is the ability of the coach to motivate his players to perform at the maximum of ability 100 per cent of the time. If the coach has the ability to do this and has his share of good talent, which is developed basically in high school and recruited and refined in college, then victory will be imminent.

Index